WINGS OF FIRE

THE OFFICIAL HOW TO DRAW

BASED ON THE SERIES BY TUI T. SUTHERLAND
ART BY BRIANNA C. WALSH
TEXT BY MARIA S. BARBO

ISBN 978-93-54716-41-6

Printed in India at Sterling Graphics Pvt. Ltd., Manesar

First printing 2023

This reprint edition April 2026

Book design by Katie Fitch and Cheung Tai

SCHOLASTIC INC.

CONTENTS

YOUR WINGS OF FIRE DRAWING JOURNEY IS ABOUT TO TAKE FLIGHT!

This book will show you how to draw twenty-five of the fiercest, friendliest, most world-changing dragons in Pyrrhia and Pantala — plus one lovable sloth!

What you'll need:

- Pencils
- Erasers
- Scrap paper
- Nicer drawing paper

You may also want:

- A pencil sharpener
- A sketchbook
- A ruler
- A thin black marker
- Colored pencils, crayons, markers, and/or watercolors!

SOME THINGS TO KNOW ABOUT THIS BOOK:

Drawing dragons may seem as challenging as ending the War of SandWing Succession, but every dragon drawing starts with the same simple shapes. And you just keep building from there — line by line, step-by-step, one shape attaching to another, until you're ready to add details and scales! Even the most complicated drawing of a NightWing starts with a group of circles, rectangles, and squiggly lines!

HERE IS SOME ANCIENT DRAWING WISDOM THAT'S BEEN PASSED AMONG THE TRIBES FOR GENERATIONS:

- Always warm up on scrap paper first. Practice drawing different kinds of lines and shapes. Move your whole arm as you draw so you don't get stiff!
- When you start a drawing, keep your lines light and loose so you can correct and erase them later on.
- Keep your grip on your pencil loose as well. It's hard to take risks and figure out fixes when your whole body is tense.
- Don't be afraid to make a messy drawing. Mistakes are part of the process!
- When you draw, think about the dragon as a whole instead of focusing on one tiny talon at a time. Drawing is like slowly zooming in on something. Start with the biggest shapes and get more detailed as you go along. That way you won't end up with the perfect face on a head that's too small for the body.
- Tracing isn't cheating! It's a good way to figure out how all the lines and shapes connect to one another.

THE NEW LINES IN EACH STEP WILL BE BLUE.

LINES THAT ARE READY TO BE ERASED WILL BE RED.

BREAK IT DOWN!

FOCUS ON THE FACE:

- Start with the outline of the eye. It makes it easier to visualize the rest of the face.
- To finish an eye, draw a tiny circle inside a larger circle. Then shade in the larger circle.
- Dragons have sharp teeth. A scalloped line can show that and save you from having to draw each tiny tooth.

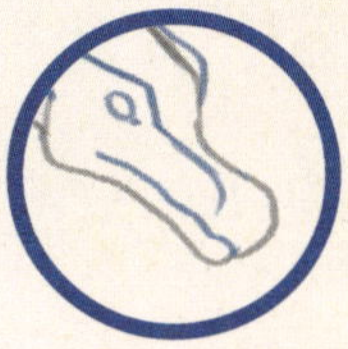

- A closed mouth starts with a straight line or a squiggly line.
- Nostrils are fun little curves!

- Dragons have lots of lines on their faces. See that line above the eye? The brow line positions both the brow and nostril — *and* sets the side of the face apart from the forehead and snout.

- Some lines are decorative and others show you where to draw the scales! (But scales themselves are details, so draw them last!) Others show off lumps or bumps.

TIPS FOR TALONS:

Start with the basic shape of a hand or foot. This will show you where to draw the talons. You can use quick lines like a stick figure hand to figure out where you want to draw each talon.

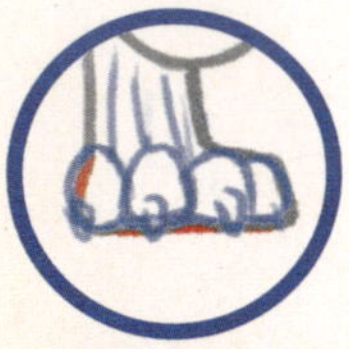

See how the talons fit inside the basic shape? Each talon starts with a vertical line. At the bottom of the line, draw a curved line. It usually looks like a lowercase letter "n." Draw one, then another, and another.

At the end of the curve is a claw. Claws are mostly triangles with rounded corners.

Now that you know the basics, are you ready to discover your own Wings of Fire?

Remember, you may not draw the perfect dragon on the first try — or even the tenth — but stick with it! Dragonets have to practice shooting venom, breathing fire, and catching prey. They have lots of mishaps! But they always learn something along the way. And you will, too!

GET READY TO SOAR!

BUMBLEBEE

This HiveWing dragonet may be smaller than a coconut, but she has a fierce spirit and a mind of her own. Are you ready to set your mind on tackling this drawing? The secret is to break it down into lots of small steps. Here's how!

1 Start by drawing a large circle for the body.

2 Now draw a diagonal line above the circle.

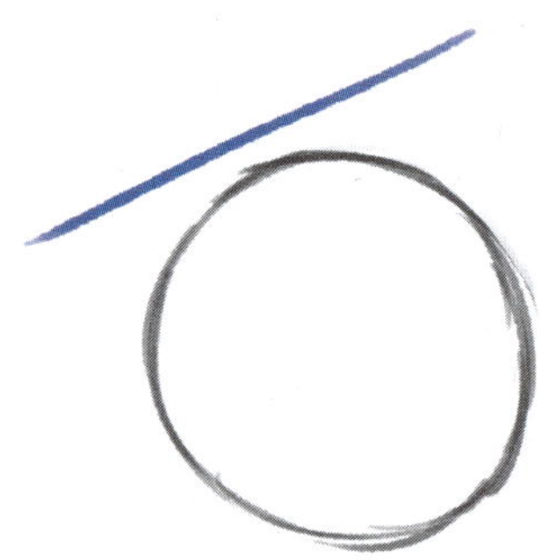

3 Draw a smaller circle at each end of the diagonal line. One is for the head, and one is for the backside.

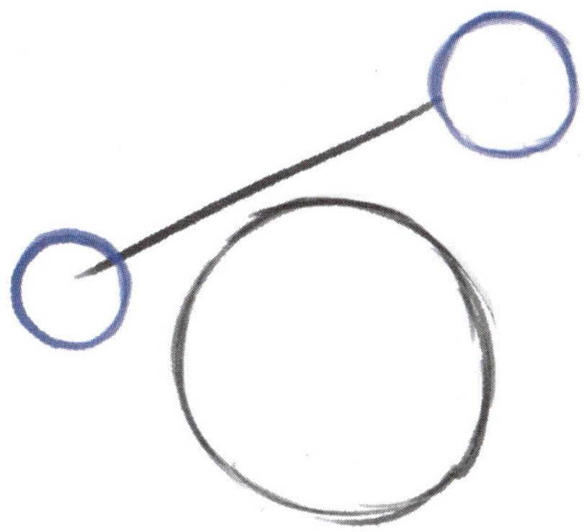

4 Connect the two smaller circles with a squiggly line. One end of the line shows the bend of the neck. The other end curves around to shape the tail.

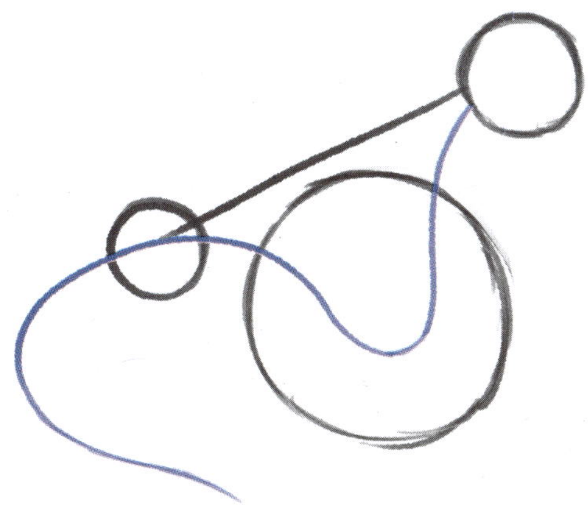

5 Use a curved line to turn the circle you drew for the body into an egg shape.

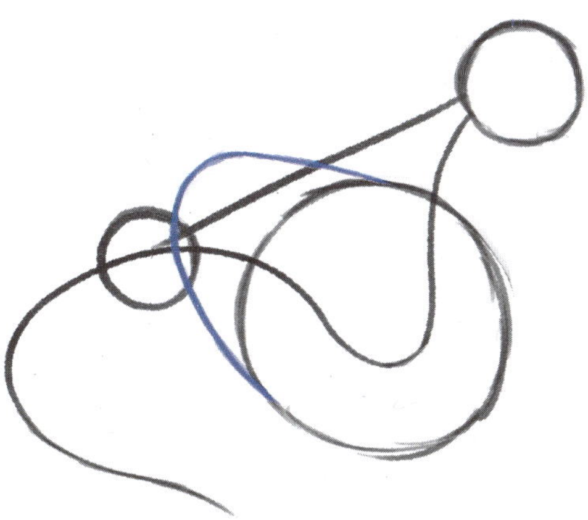

6 Connect the head to the egg-shaped body with two curved lines. Can you see the neck starting to take shape?

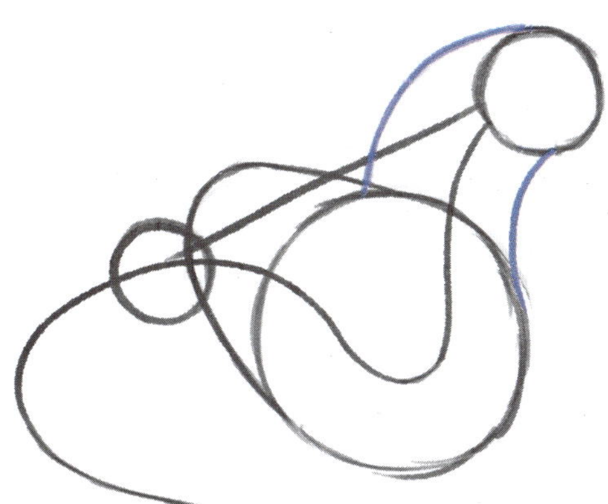

7 Attach a tail to the circle you drew for the backside.

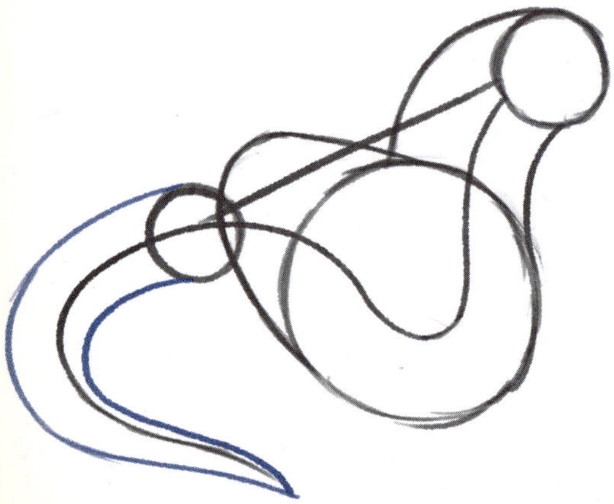

8 Sketch in the basic shapes of that back leg. Keep your lines light and loose for now. You'll clean them up later.

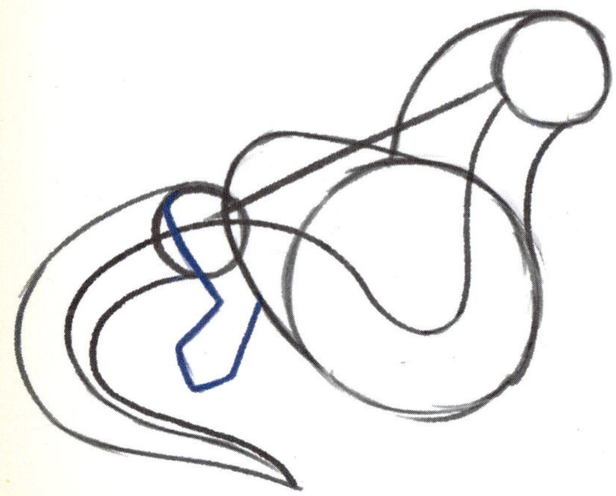

9 Now lightly sketch in the left front leg. Start with two angled lines, then draw a triangular shape at the end.

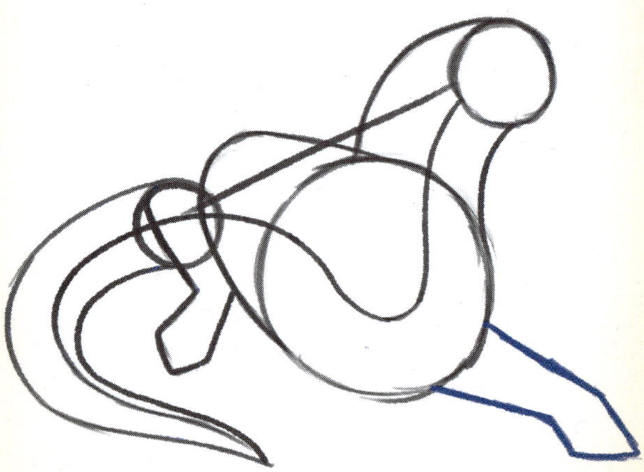

10 Wing it! Draw a shape that looks like a plane's wing behind the body. This will be one of Bumblebee's segmented wings.

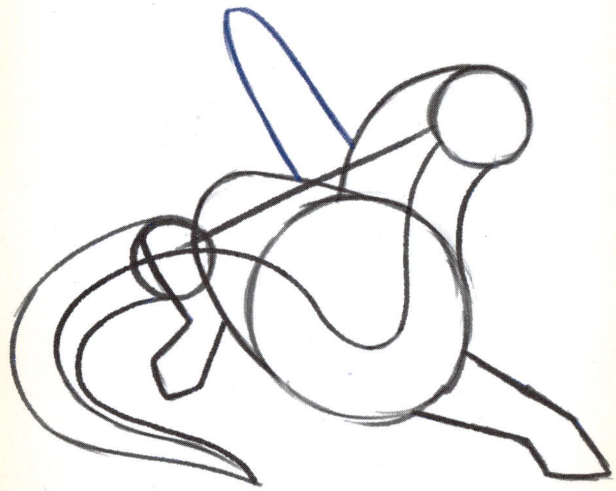

11 Use a curved line to tuck another wing behind it.

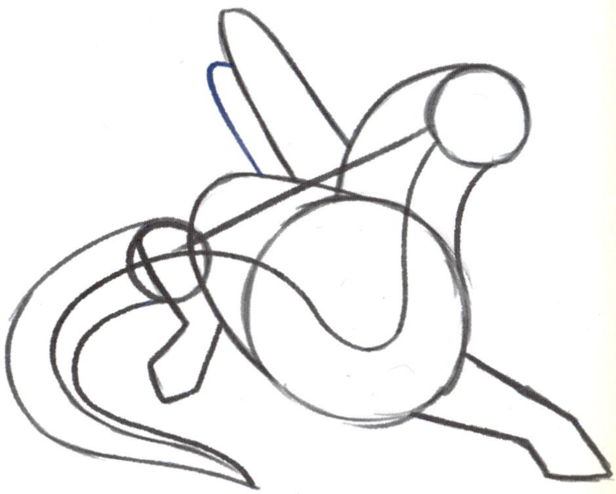

12 Ready to draw the head? Use the circle you drew in step 3 as a guide. Then break the head down into basic shapes — two rectangles and a triangle. Now draw two antennae, one coming out of the point of the triangle and one coming out of the base.

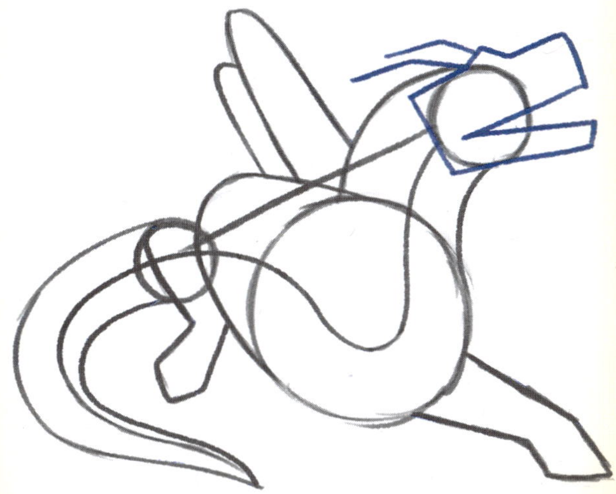

13 Bumblebee's ears are pushed back like a dog who wants to play! Sketch in the shape of the front ear. It looks kind of like a spearhead or a diamond.

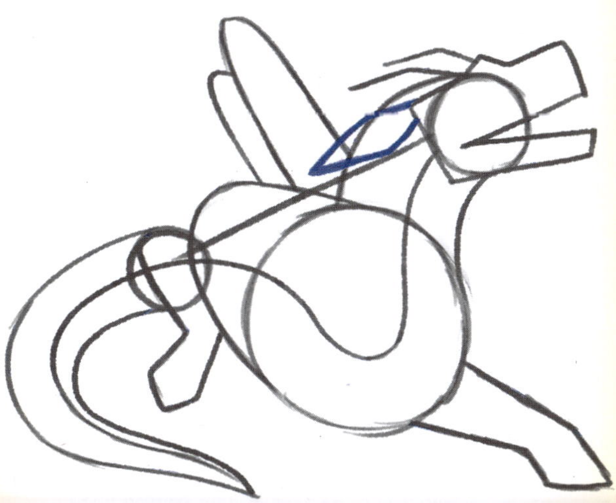

14 Use a series of ovals and straight lines to block in the right front leg. (Later you'll connect the outlines of these basic shapes to create the leg.)

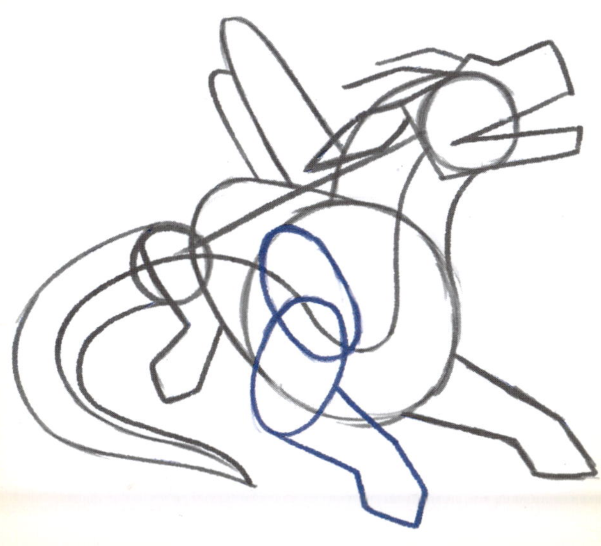

15

More wings! Bumblebee's right wings connect to the top oval of the leg you drew in step 14. Use long "U" shapes to sketch in the front wings. See how they connect to the leg oval?

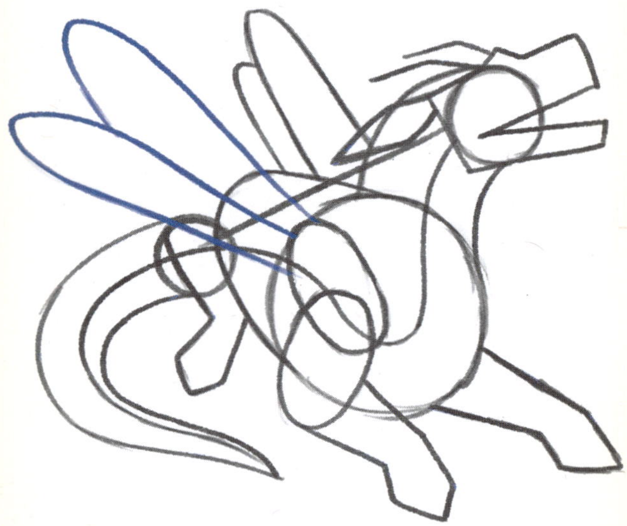

16

Now take a minute to clean up the outlines. Then check the angles and proportions. Do all the shapes connect just how you want them to? Are Bumblebee's left wings smaller than her right wings? Great! See all those red lines? Go ahead and erase them. You won't need them to guide you anymore!

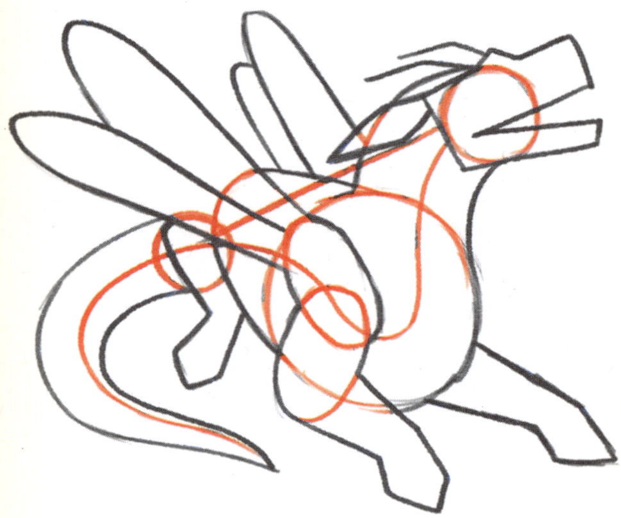

17

Detail time! Let's start with the head. Sketch in the outline of the eye. Above the eye, draw a curved line that follows the curve of the top of the head. Then use jagged lines for the teeth.

The antennae you drew in step 12 are the tops of the horns. Go ahead and sketch in the bottoms of the horns. Then erase any lines you don't need.

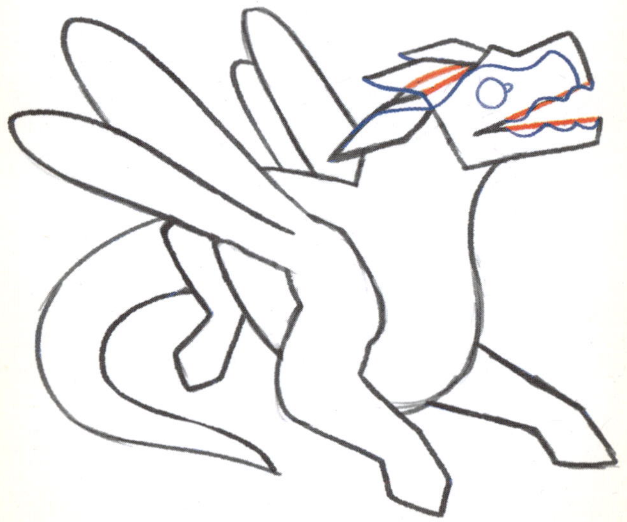

18

Add another layer of detail. Fill in the pupil and draw the nostril. Add a curved line inside the mouth for the tongue. Then clean up the edges of the shoulder and snout. Is Bumblebee's nose horn taking shape? Add stripes to the ear, then focus the wings. Draw curved lines that follow the top edge of each wing. Finish up by erasing extra lines.

19 This step is all about short, curved lines. Use them in the wings to add details and to refine the shape of the ears and forehead. Draw a curve inside the elbow so the front leg looks like it's bending. Then start shaping the dragon's toes.

20 Wing it! Double up the lines you drew on the wings in step 19 to outline Bumblebee's yellow stripes. Then sketch in some guidelines on the body. These will help you draw the scales in the next two steps. Don't forget to draw a triangle for each tearing talon!

21 Almost done! Keep building up the details with short, curved lines and continue to refine the edges. Then get started on the scales! Use the guidelines you drew in step 20 to draw a row of upside-down triangles on the neck and tail.

22 Scale up! Use the guidelines you drew in steps 20 and 21 to draw this dragon's protective scales. Notice all the curved lines on the legs and wings. See all the loose rectangles on the neck and tail? What shapes do you see in the scales on Bumblebee's body and face?

KINKAJOU

Kinkajou is a RainWing dragon to remember. And she does not let anything hold her back — especially not other dragons who want to tell her what to do! So what if her venom doesn't actually hit the leaf target? Kinkajou will just keep trying until she's spot-on.

Practice makes progress for dragons and drawings. Are you up for the challenge?

1 Start by drawing a circle for Kinkajou's body/chest — just like you did for Bumblebee.

2 Draw a short diagonal line above the circle and to the right.

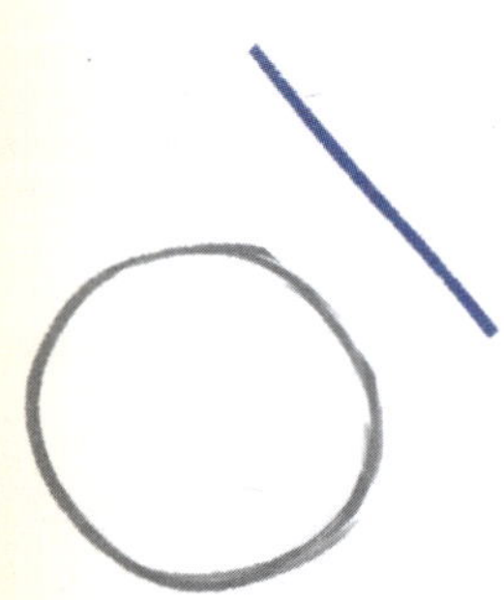

3 Draw a small circle at each end of the line — one for the head and one for the tail/backside. The circle for the head should be slightly larger.

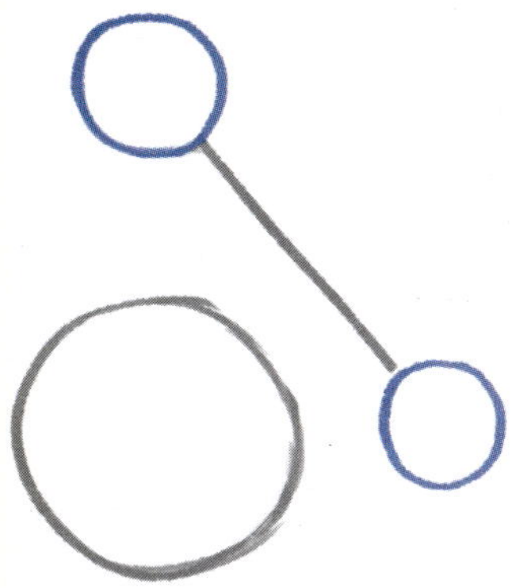

4 Draw a swerving line that runs through all three circles. This line is longer than the one you drew for Bumblebee because Kinkajou's tail is longer and spirals at the end.

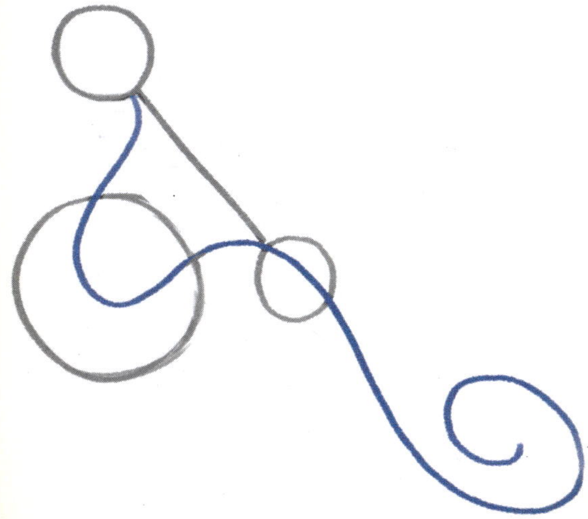

5 Use two curved lines to connect the large body/chest circle to the circle you drew for the tail end. Kinkajou's body curves around a little more than Bumblebee's.

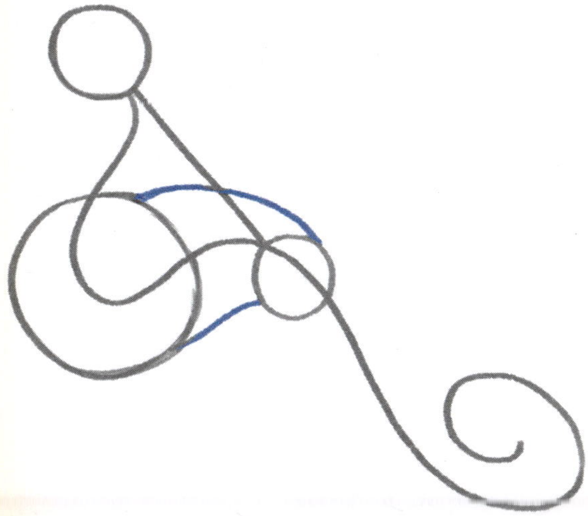

6 Use two more curves to widen and shape the neck.

7 Keep at it! Kinkajou never gives up, even when things get challenging. Follow her lead and use the same technique you used in step 6 to fill out Kinkajou's tail.

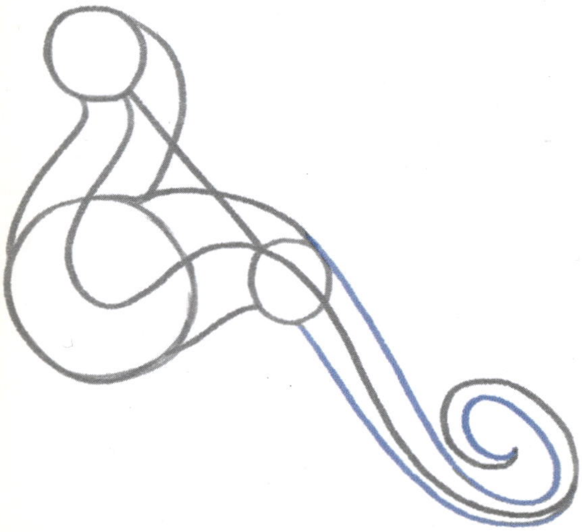

8 Roughly sketch in two legs, keeping your lines light, loose, and boxy. Don't worry about getting it perfect at this stage. All you need is a sense of where each leg's position is and the general shape.

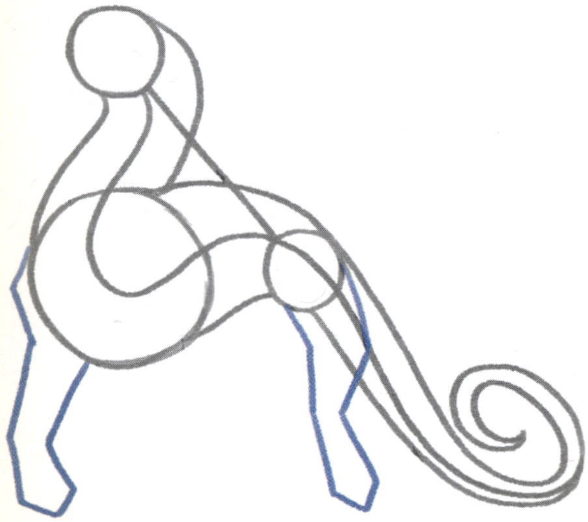

9 Where will you draw the wing? Sketch in some starter lines to guide you. You can use a right angle if you want to make that top angle extra sharp.

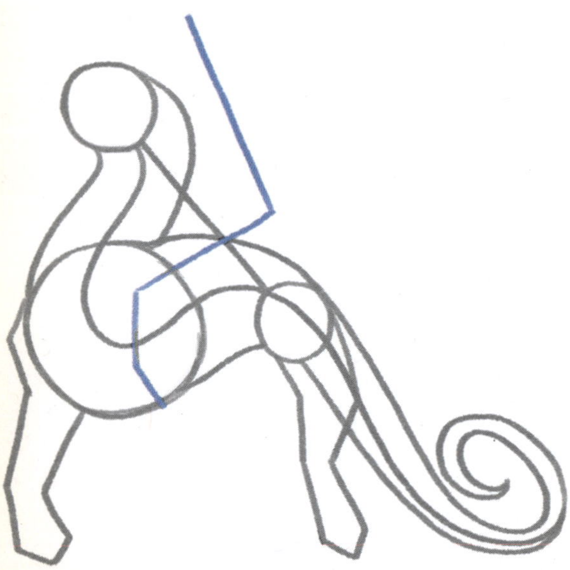

10 Every part of this dragon drawing connects to another part of the drawing. Now that you know where the wing goes, you can draw the other front leg. See how the back of the leg connects to the wing bone?

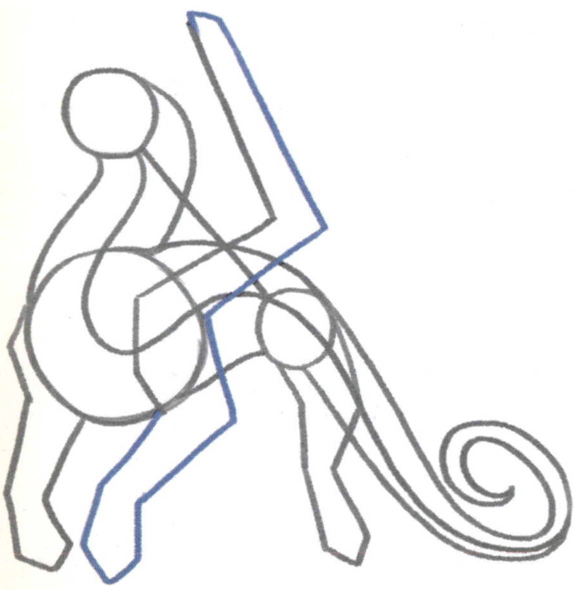

11 Sketch in the basic shapes of the head: two rectangles and a diamond for the ear.

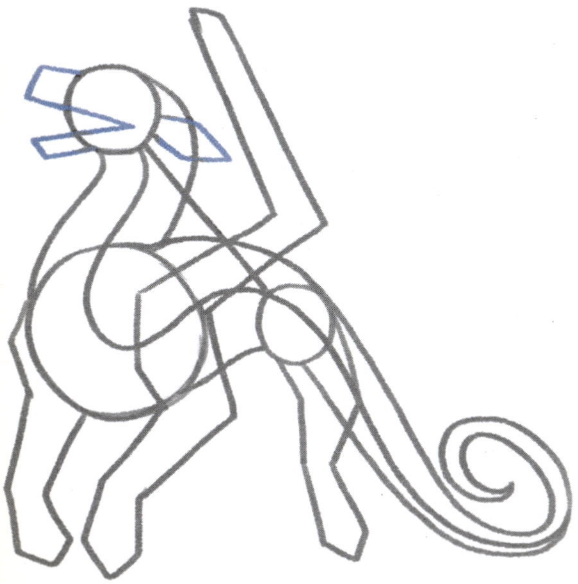

12 Use curved lines to attach the wings to the starter shapes you drew in steps 9 and 10.

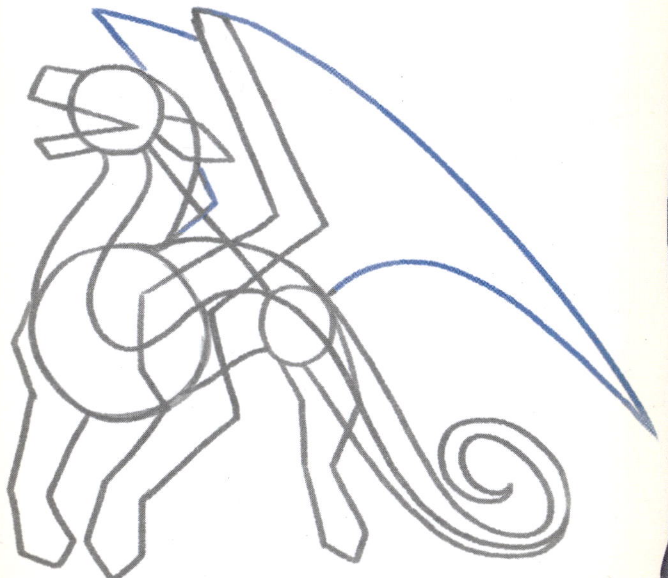

13 Use upside-down "V" shapes to block in the talons on top of the wings. Then sketch in the back leg. Pay attention to the places where the lines meet. Where does the back leg sit in relation to the front leg?

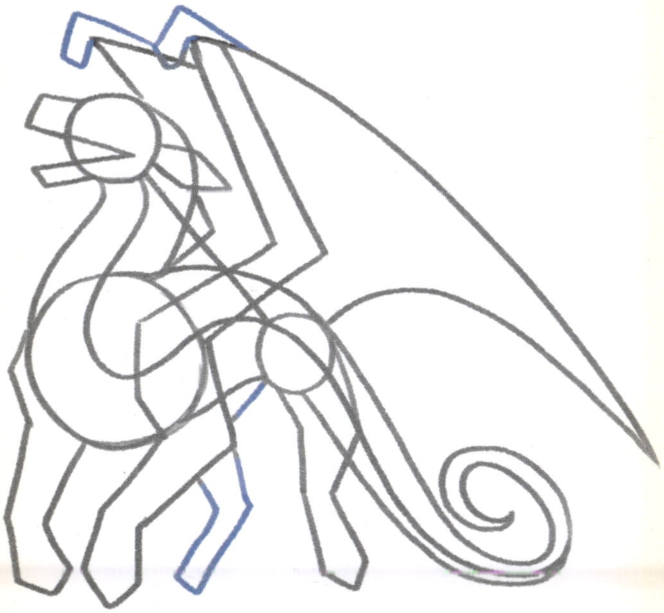

14 Erase any lines you don't need. Then step back and take a look at your drawing before adding details. Are all the shapes where you need them to be?

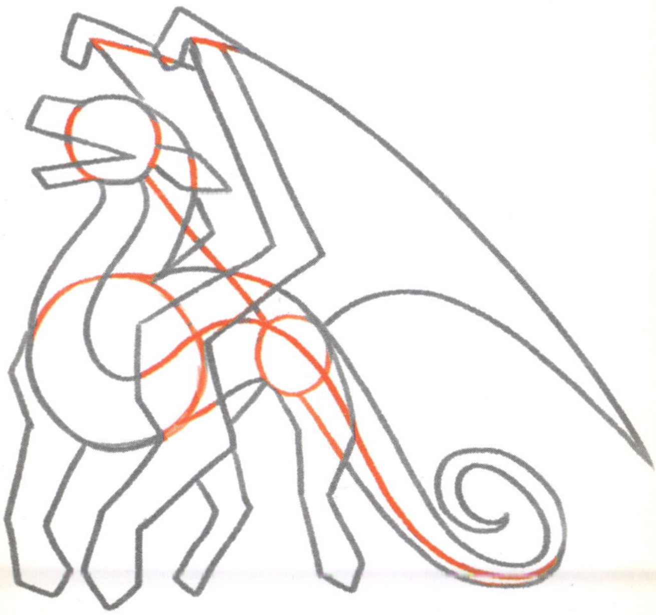

15 Face time! Start by drawing the horn on Kinkajou's snout, then sketch the outline of the eye. Does drawing the face feel tricky? Try tracing the lines on scrap paper first to get a feel for where they go.

16 Keep adding details to the face — like the ruff that fans out behind every RainWing's ears. Fill in the pupil in the eye, draw a nostril, and then adjust the shape of the jaw, hind leg, and front leg.

17 Using the lines you've already drawn as a guide, start to reshape the front talons. Then work on the wings! Add a talon to the top of each wing and another extending out of the elbow joint. Then draw a long line down the middle of the left wing.

18 Watch out for those talons! Keep adding details to the talons and wings. Use simple, curved lines to form the bottom of the wings and the bony elbow. Use pointy triangles to make each talon sharp.

19 Practice makes progress! Slowly build up the details like the bend in the elbow, Kinkajou's sharp teeth, more wing bones, and the edges of the wings. How many different kinds of lines do you see in this step?

20 In this step, you'll draw guidelines that will make it easier to add Kinkajou's scales. Here's a tip: Most of these new lines run parallel to lines you've already drawn.

21 Use short, horizontal lines, like stripes, to draw the scales. Then erase every other edge until you see rows of rectangles. Remember, you don't have to draw every scale. A few carefully placed lines will make a dragon look as if it's covered in scales!

22 RainWing scales shift colors to reflect their moods and to blend into their surroundings. What colors will you choose to show off Kinkajou's bright mood?

TSUNAMI

Do not mess with Tsunami. This SeaWing is a force! She's always known she was destined to be in charge, but being the SeaWing queen feels too restrictive. Teaching battle moves, on the other hand? That's fun! Just like drawing this dragon.

1 Start with a large circle.

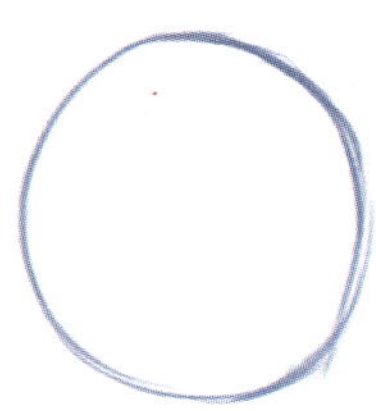

2 Then draw a diagonal line through one-third of it.

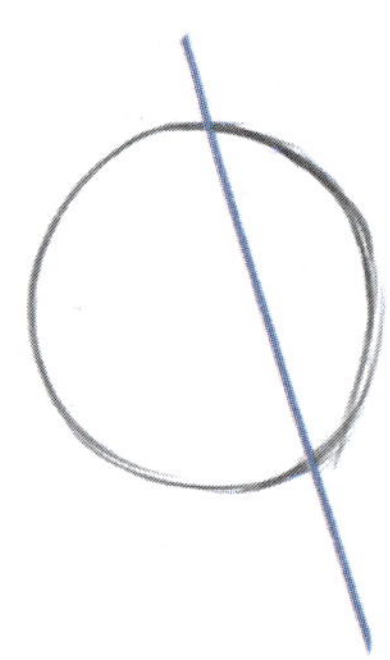

3 Draw a circle at each end of the line. Make the bottom circle twice as big as the top one.

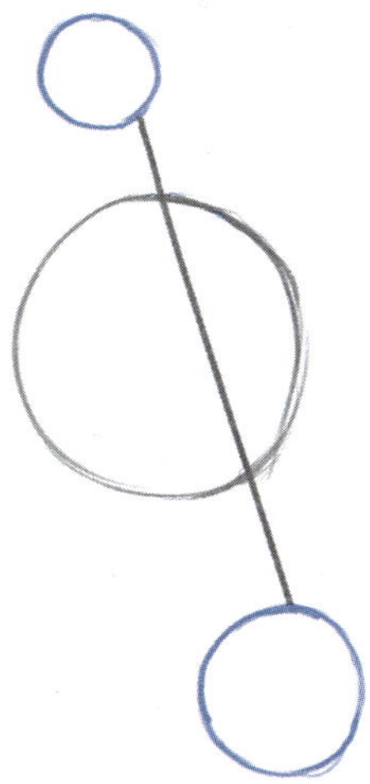

4 Connect the two smaller circles with a flowing line that travels through the circle you drew for the body. This is Tsunami's spine. Notice the bend of the neck and the curve of the tail.

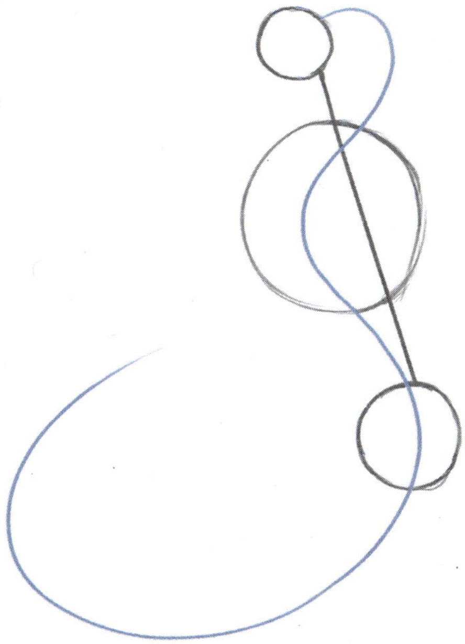

5 Time to build on the skeleton you drew in step 4. Use it as a guide to widen the neck and upper tail.

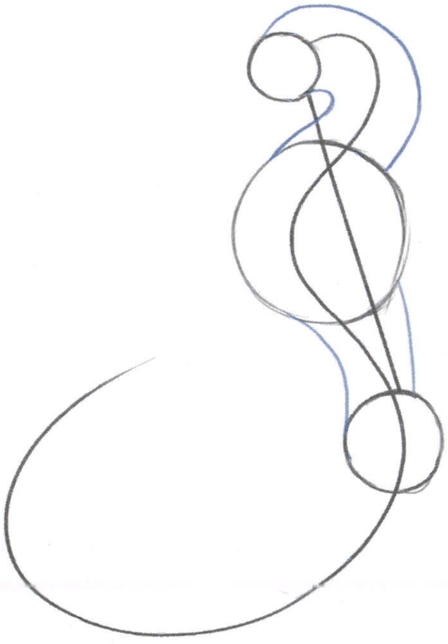

6 Use the spine as a guide to shape the tail. See how the inner curved line is much shorter than the outer one?

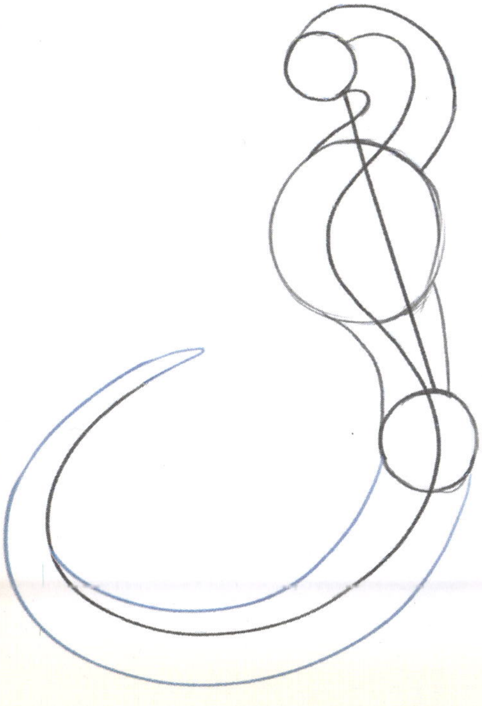

7 Draw an oval for the shoulder. The top edge lines up with the top edge of the body circle. Then draw the basic shapes of the forearm, hand, and elbow.

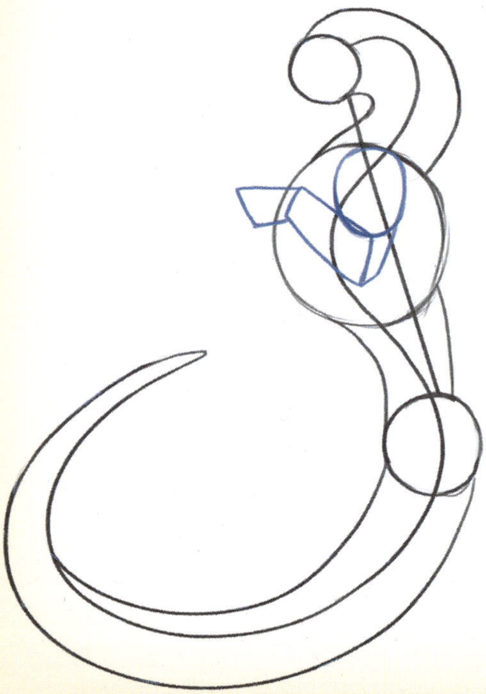

8 Sketch the back leg around the circle you drew in step 3. A curved "U" shape at the top forms a knee. A straight line at the back defines the leg. At this stage, the foot looks like a flipper.

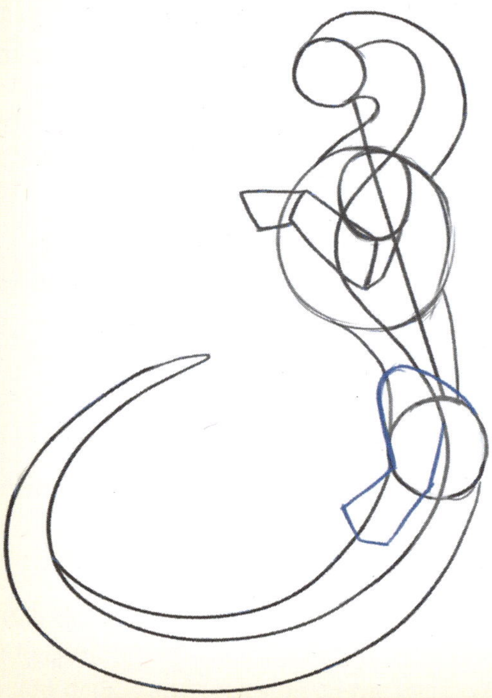

9 Think about the lines that make up the right arm. A curved line for the shoulder, a right angle for the elbow, a hand that looks like a hoof. Then set up the wing using a circle and a "V" shape.

10 Tsunami's wings look regal in this drawing. Draw a loose outline using curved lines at the sides and straight lines at the top. Then use three straight lines to set the right leg behind the left.

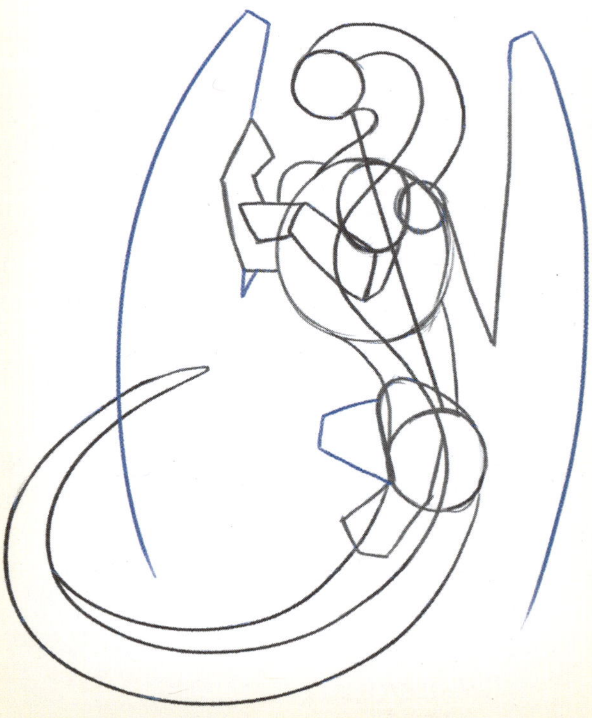

11 Lightly sketch in the basic shapes of Tsunami's horns, snout, and jaw. Her head looks like a dog's head at this stage. Then used curved lines to attach the bottoms of the wings.

12 Add a diamond-shaped ear. Then draw a long line on each wing. Use straight, parallel lines to draw the wing bones. Can you imagine Tsunami using them to open and close her powerful wings?

13 Use curved lines to add fins to her chest and the back of her neck and tail. Then close off the bottom of her right wing.

14 Congrats! You've sketched in all the basic shapes of the body! Now erase any lines you no longer need and take a minute to check the proportions.

15 Focus on the face! Draw the outline of the eye. Use scalloped lines and curves to shape the jaw, forehead, and snout. Erase old guidelines as you go along.

16 Draw the pupil in the upper corner of the eye to show Tsunami's playful side. Clean up the outlines of the neck and jaw. Then add points to her neck fins and elliptical shapes under her chin.

17 Use short, straight lines to add details to the neck fins and to set up the fins on her chest. Then add sharp teeth, a nostril, and the detail line on her forehead.

18 Talon time! Draw them just like you did for the other dragons. Then add webbing in between each one for superfast deep-sea swimming! Finish by sketching in the fins.

19 Use curved lines to reshape the outlines of the legs. Then tackle those talons! Don't forget the talon at the top of each wing.

20 Draw scalloped fins on the back of Tsunami's tail and talons on her right foot. Then add structure to the wings with long, curved lines and pointed, taloned ends.

21 Almost there! Draw a curve/bump at each joint in the wings. Add a scalloped edge to the bottom of the back wing. Then take a step back. What finishing touches does this dragon need?

22 Get ready for color! This aquatic dragon slays the sea in shades of royal blue and emerald green. Use highlights in lighter shades to show off the scales that light up when she speaks in the SeaWings' secret underwater language!

ANEMONE

*Sea*sational! Princess Anemone is Tsunami's sister, Queen Coral's daughter, and an animus dragon. She grew up harnessed to her mom, so when she moved to the Jade Mountain Academy, she took every opportunity to fly as fast as she wanted and soar as high as she could go. How far will you go with your new drawing skills?

1 Start with two circles — a small one for the head and a larger one for the body.

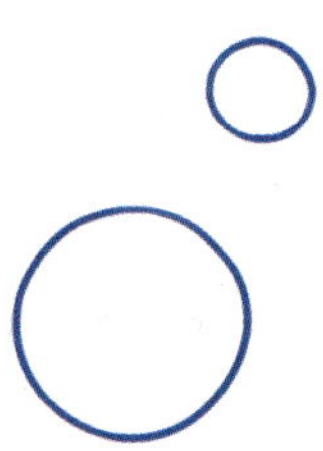

2 Attach the basic shapes of the snout and horn to the head circle.

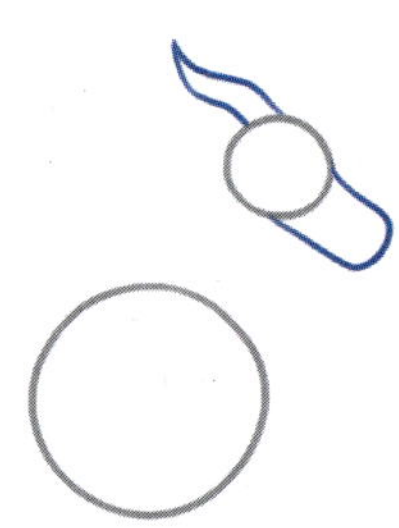

3 Draw Anemone's neck with two curved lines. Then start the tail with one big, sweeping curve.

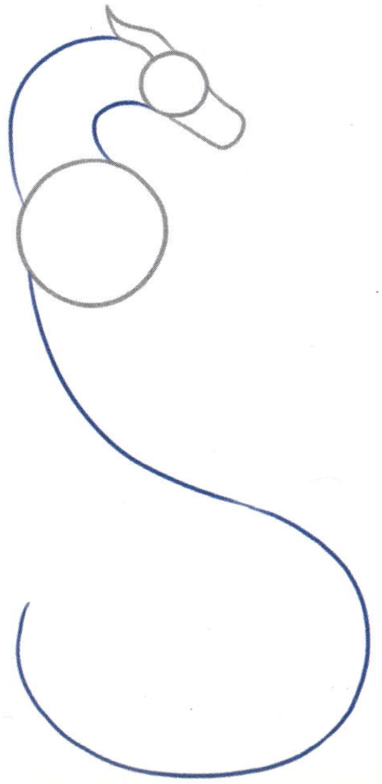

4 Finish the tail with another curved line that runs parallel to the first.

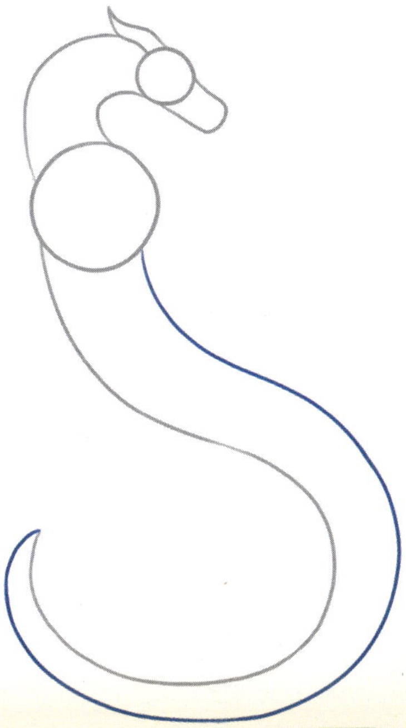

5 Sketch in the basic shapes of the upper arm, forearm, and hand. Then notice where the wing attaches to the upper arm. Draw a starter line to set up that wing!

6 Finish Anemone's right wing. Use two curved lines for the sides and a scalloped edge for the bottom. Then lightly sketch in the basic shapes of the leg. A sideways "U" forms the thigh, and a rounded triangle will become the foot.

7

Keep building up your drawing! Use a curve to tuck the left leg behind the right. Add another curve above the right arm to show the left. Draw the ear. Then sketch in a framework for the left wing — one right angle and a curve!

8

Remember the scalloped fins you drew on Tsunami's chest? Draw them on Anemone now. Then use the same kind of lines for the bottom of the wing. Ready to start on the face? Draw an eye, curved brow, and a squiggly line for the mouth. Then shape the bottom curve of the jaw.

9

Erase the red lines. Is your drawing starting to look like a SeaWing princess? Take some time to fix any lines, angles, and shapes that need reworking.

10

Dive deep into details! Draw fins on the back of Anemone's neck, and add the left wing bone. It looks kind of like the letter "Y." Then draw a curved guideline on the neck. This will help you draw the scales on the underside of her neck.

11 Ready for more details? Draw one talon on top of each wing and three on her left hand. Add a curved line inside the ear to give it depth. Then draw two barbs on her chin and a curved line on the jaw that connects to the guideline you drew in step 10.

12 Step back and look at your drawing. What does it need? Talons on the left hand and right foot? Draw them now! Then use four curved lines to add structure and dimension to her left wing.

13 Did you know SeaWings can breathe underwater? Draw a column of "V" shapes on Anemone's neck for gills. Add fins to the back of her tail. Then use a series of curved lines to add dimension to the wing and tail.

14 Time for finishing touches! Clean up your outlines and add scales to Anemone's face and tail. Anemone's wings are a pale white-pink, like the inside of seashells. Will you use markers, colored pencils, or paints to color them in?

CORAL

Queen Coral of the SeaWings is also the super-protective mom of Tsunami, Anemone, and Auklet. Can you see the family resemblance? Coral's regal pose is similar to Anemone's. Drawing dragons in similar-but-different poses is a great way to practice new skills. What have you learned from drawing her daughters that you can apply to this drawing of the queen?

1 Start with a circle for the chest.

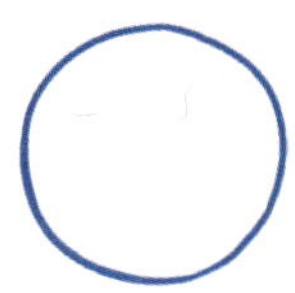

2 Above the circle, draw a rectangular shape for her face. It is slightly wider at the forehead than it is at the chin.

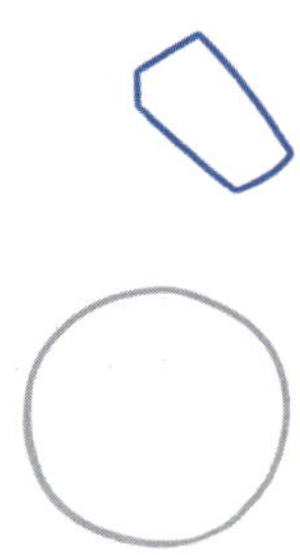

3 Connect those shapes with two curved lines for the neck.

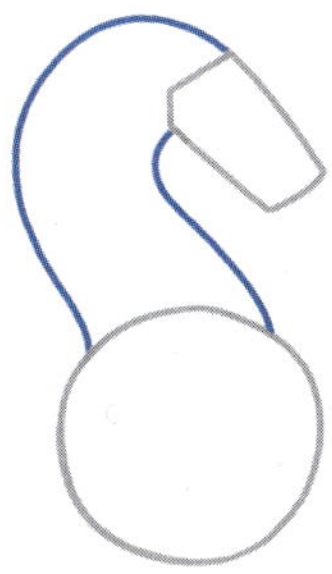

4 Draw two ovals for Coral's strong upper arms. You can't see the whole shape of the left arm because it is tucked behind her body.

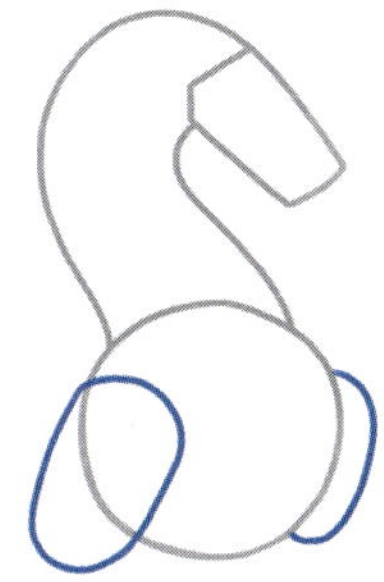

5 Sketch in two longer ovals for the forearms and add the basic shape of her right hand. Then draw a bean shape below her upper body. It should not touch any other shapes or stick out farther than her elbow. This will become Coral's bent right leg.

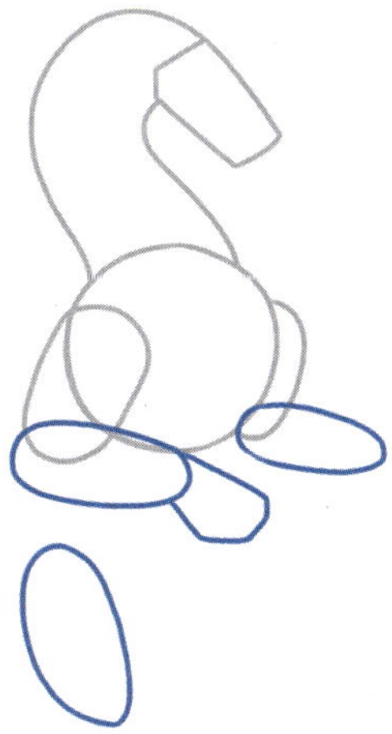

6 Back to basics! Draw the starter shapes of the left hand and right foot. Then use two sweeping lines to sketch in the tail! Do you see the way the leg sits entirely inside the tail?

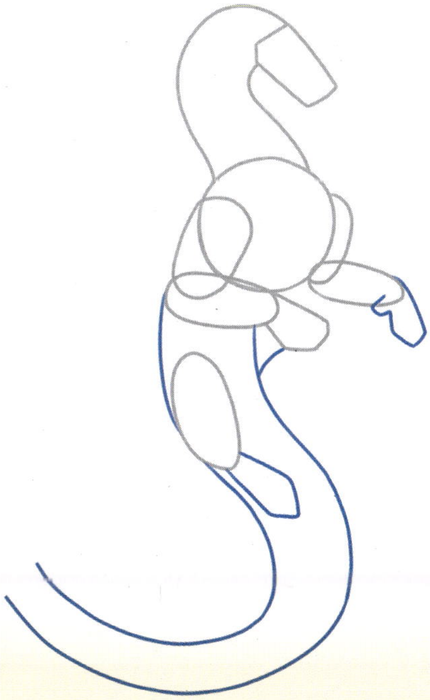

7 Where do the wings attach to the body? Use light, loose lines to position the wings. At this stage, they look almost like the letter "W."

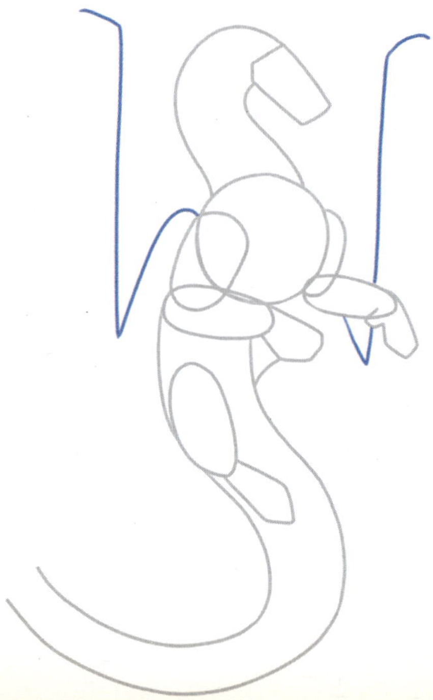

8 Finish up the shapes of the legs and wings. Use two long curves for the sides of the wings. The bottom edges of each wing are pointed, scalloped lines just like the ones you used for Tsunami and Anemone.

9 Face time! Draw the outline of the eye, and then sketch a squiggly line above it from the snout to the tip of the horn. Finish the horns and draw the mouth, ear, and talon on the tip of her wing.

10 Take a minute to check your outlines and erase any lines you no longer need. Does Queen Coral's tail swoop behind her right wing? Do her wings protect her on two sides like shields? Then you're good to go!

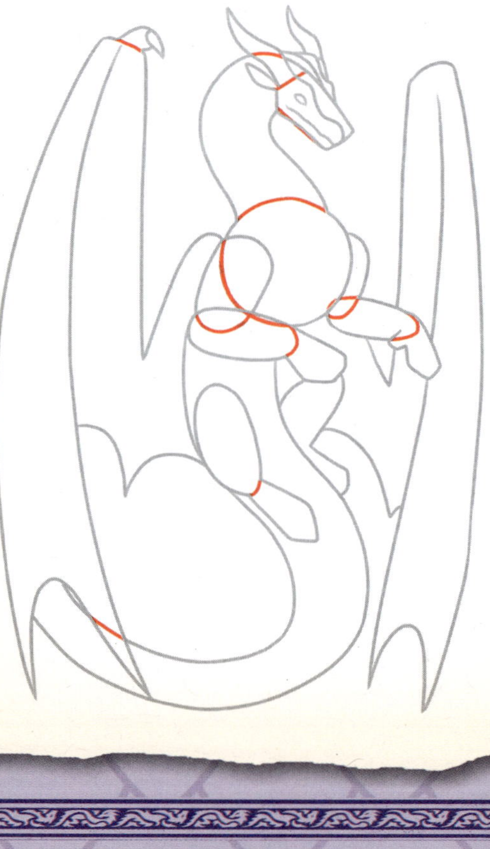

11 Draw the talon at the top of her left wing. Then add details to her eyes and two ovals at the base of her chin. Refine the shape of her forearms and start adding talons to her right hand. Don't forget to draw the webbing between her talons.

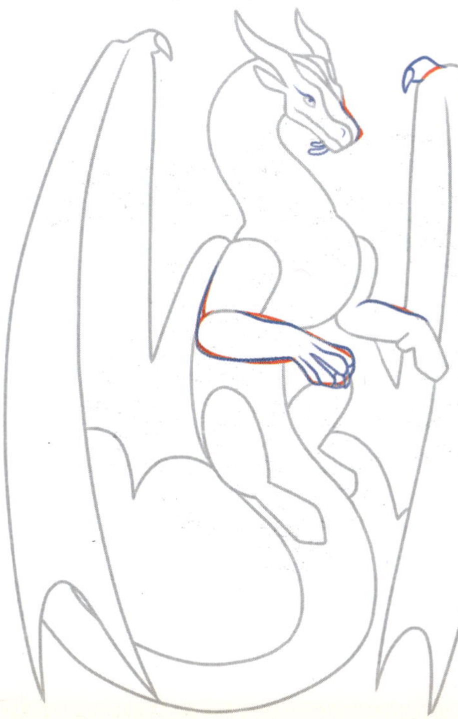

12 Draw a curved line in each leg to make them look bent. Then continue tackling those talons. Trace her left hand on scrap paper first to get a feel for the way the lines come together. What kinds of lines and shapes do you see in the hand?

13 Use scalloped lines to draw the fins on Coral's neck and chest. Then use short, curved lines to draw the band of bioluminescent scales above her eyes. When you're ready, work on the wing bones. They look like giant "V"s with a bony elbow.

14 Time for finishing touches like scales, gills, and fins. Then try drawing the strands of pearls Queen Coral wears. Now that you can draw Queen Coral, imagine drawing her swimming!

AUKLET

Now that you can draw the rest of the SeaWing royal family, shake things up with this drawing of the youngest royal sister getting ready to have a snack. Auklet hatched safely thanks to her big sister Tsunami, who fought off an animus-enchanted statue that was trying to smash her egg. What's keeping you from smashing this drawing?

1 Draw a large circle for the body near the middle of your paper. Then draw an egg shape for the turtle's body in the lower right-hand corner of your paper.

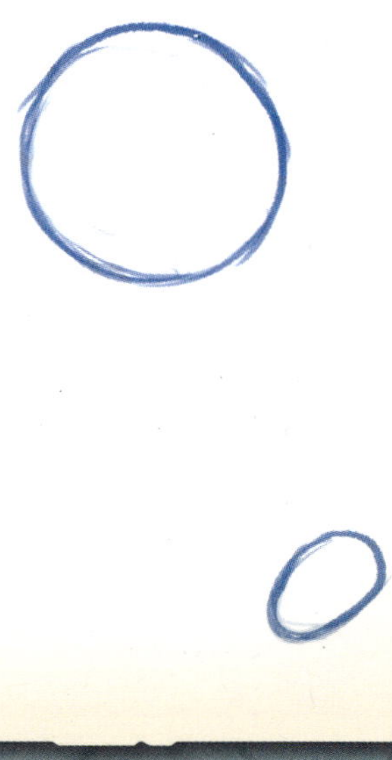

2 Squint your eyes to blur the lines of the drawing and help you see the basic shapes of the head, neck, and tail. Then draw them around the circle you drew in step 1. Make sure the mouth is open and ready to chomp. Do you see the way Auklet's whole body curves into a lowercase "n"? She really wants that turtle!

3 What basic shapes do you see in the legs? Here's a hint: They're similar to the starter shapes you used for Anemone. Draw them, then add two lines inside the mouth to make it look three-dimensional. Finish up with a small circle for the shoulder and another one for the turtle's head.

4 The arms and wings will both extend out of the shoulder circle you drew in step 3. Sketch in their basic lines and shapes. Pay attention to the angle of the upper arm. It looks like it's tucked into the body. Then start adding facial features. Finish up by giving the turtle four flippers.

5 Block in the left arm. Notice the way it peeks out from behind Auklet's right arm. Wing time! Choose a starting point like the front wing. Think about its shape and the way it connects to the two lines that extend from the shoulder circle. How does the left wing fit behind the right wing?

6 Erase the red lines and clean up your drawing.

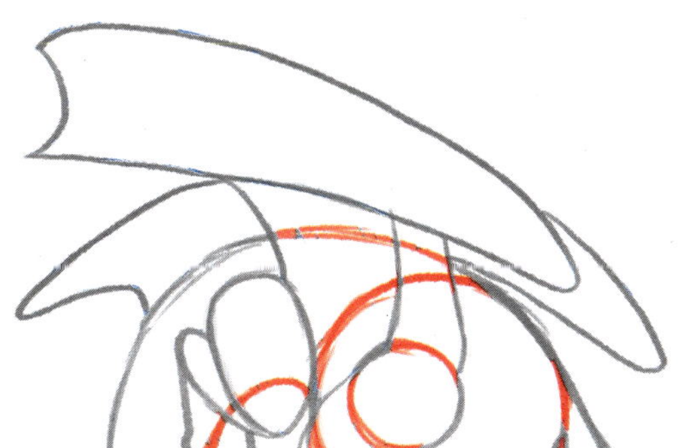

7 Ready to move on? Add smaller details like the curves of her tongue, nostril, chin scales, and left horn. Then section off the talons and draw a short, curved line from the armpit to the top of the thigh.

8 Wing bones look like long, bony fingers. Draw three on Auklet's front wing and one on her back wing. Look for the "V" shape in between each one. Then add a detail line to the ear and a dot to the turtle's head for its eye.

9 Ready to make Auklet look more like a SeaWing? Add fins to her back and scales to her neck. Draw a guideline on her tail to help you draw her scales. What other details can you add?

10 Try something different! Sometimes, you can use a few lines here and there to hint that the whole body is covered in scales. Other times, you may want to draw each scale. Don't forget the turtle has a pattern on its body, too!

CLAY

As a MudWing bigwings, Clay has a big heart and an even bigger appetite! He's always acted like a big brother to the other dragonets of destiny. And he's always had snacks on his mind. Clay is swooping down to snatch up some sparrows in this pose, so you'll be using lots of curved lines and rounded forms.

1 Draw an egg on an angle near the top of the paper. Then draw a six-sided shape for the head. The head sits below the egg-shaped body and a little to the left. Connect the shapes with a diagonal line.

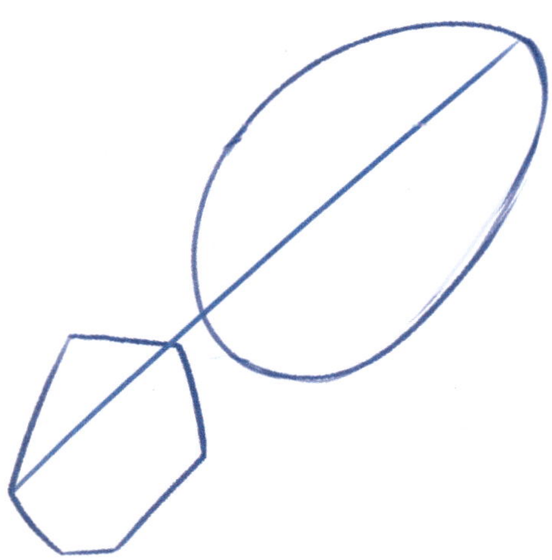

2 Draw two curved lines for Clay's thick neck. The top line is longer than the bottom line. See the way his head curves all the way down? He's on the hunt for prey! Then draw a curve for his left wing.

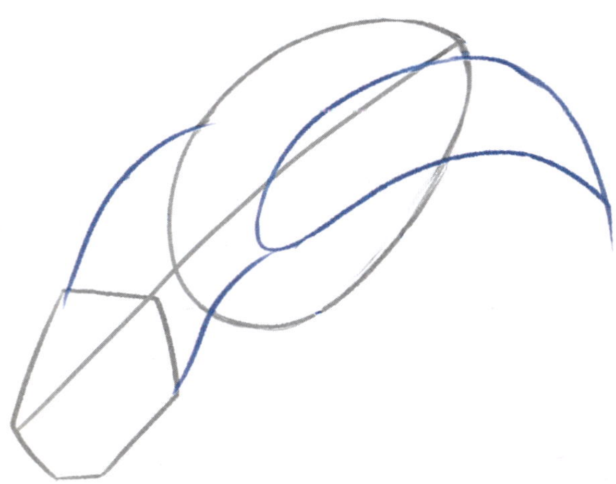

3 Draw the bottom line of the right wing. It's a long arc, like a frown that runs from the neckline to the edge of the paper. Two "U"-shaped legs peek out from under the wings, like flippers.

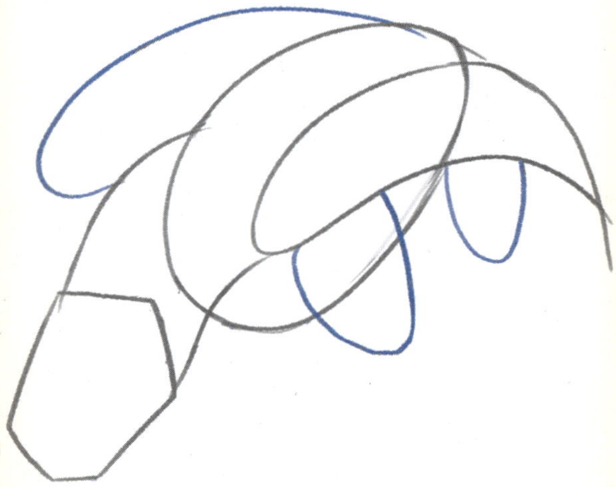

4 Attach the left arm and leg onto the starter shapes you drew in step 3. Then draw a line that drops straight down from the back of the right wing. This is the top of the tail. The bottom of the tail is almost a complete circle.

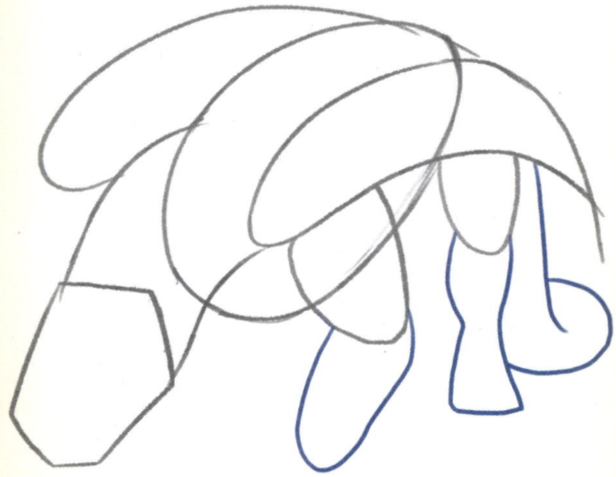

5 Clay's right forearm is straight and narrow. It's a little longer than the head and peeks out from behind it. The right leg is much smaller than the other limbs. It extends out from behind the left leg — and so does the tip of the tail!

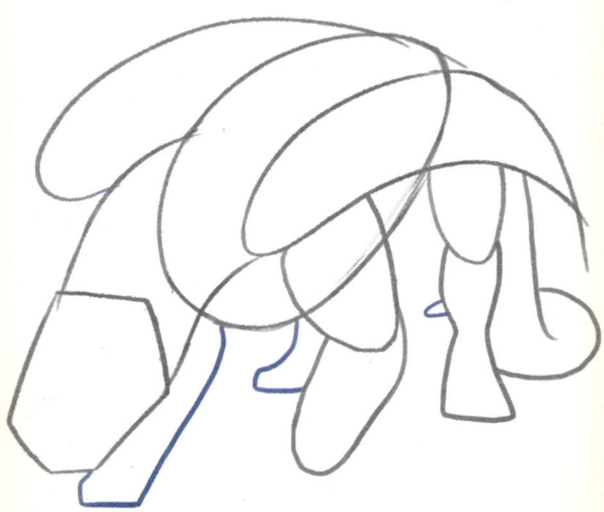

6 Unlike the other dragons you've drawn, Clay has a broad, boxy head. Use straight lines to square off his head. Then draw two ovals for the birds on the ground in front of him. Finally, add his ears, horns, and a modified "U" shape for his left foot.

7 Time for a spot check! Erase the lines you don't need. Are Clay's arms and legs taking shape? Use the boxy guidelines you drew in step 6 to help place the eyes, mouth, and nostrils. Then draw details on the birds.

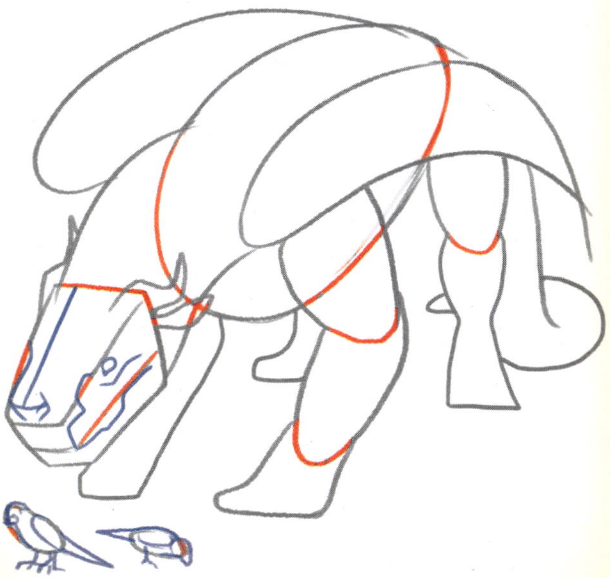

8 Draw a spine on Clay's back. You'll need this guideline in step 10. Then draw more guidelines to set up the bone structure of the wings. It's similar to the bone structure in a scavenger hand. See the bump for the joints? His wings even have talons on the ends like fingers!

9 Three . . . two . . . one . . . talons! This step is all about drawing talons. The toes are straight lines that lead into curved lines. The claws sit along the bottom edge of the starter shapes you drew in steps 4 and 5. They're shaped like triangles with rounded corners.

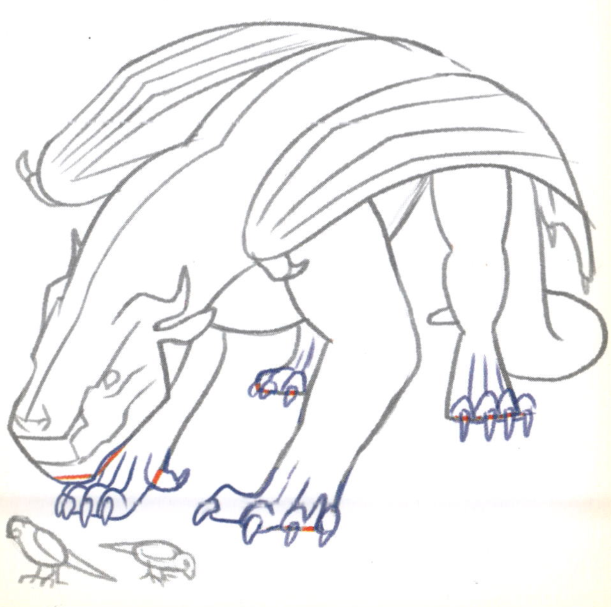

10 Ready for final details? Draw the spiky ridges along Clay's back. Add curved lines for the knee and the bend in his arm. Then draw another curve on his chest and on the outer edge of the tail to make them look more three-dimensional. Now you're ready for color!

SUNNY

Sunny radiates warmth, and it's not just because SandWing scales give off heat! Sunny sees the best in everyone. And she knows that sometimes you have to have faith that things will turn out OK — whether that thing is a prophecy or a drawing!

1 Start with a large circle for Sunny's body.

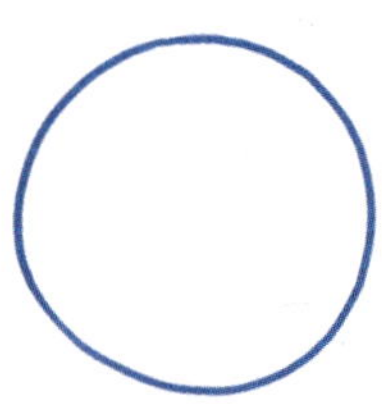

2 Draw the basic shape of Sunny's head. The back of the head is a right angle, and the mouth is a sideways "V" shape. The head sits above the circle and to the right and almost touches the edge of the paper.

3 Attach the head to the body circle with two lines. Sunny is holding her head up high, so there isn't much of a curve to her neck.

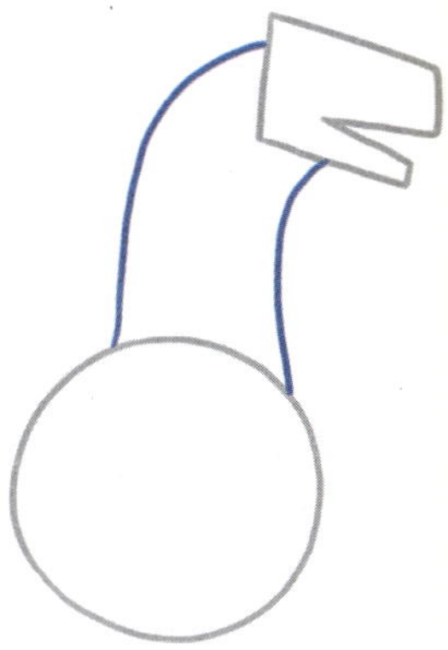

4 Draw the top section of Sunny's tail.

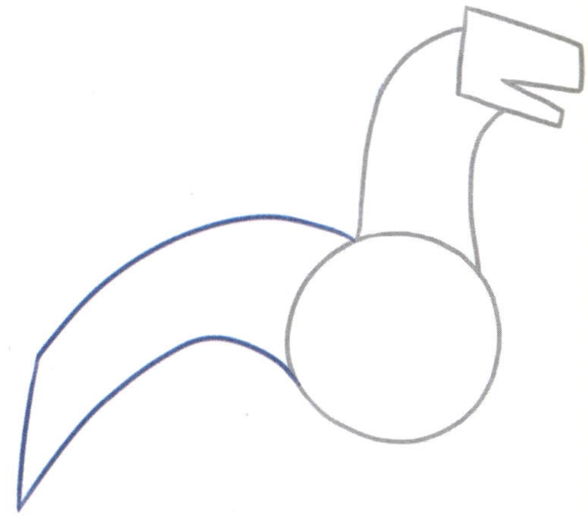

5 Draw two long ovals. One sits inside the circle you drew for the body. The other sits inside the tail.

6 Use more elliptical shapes to continue building the shape of the arm and leg.

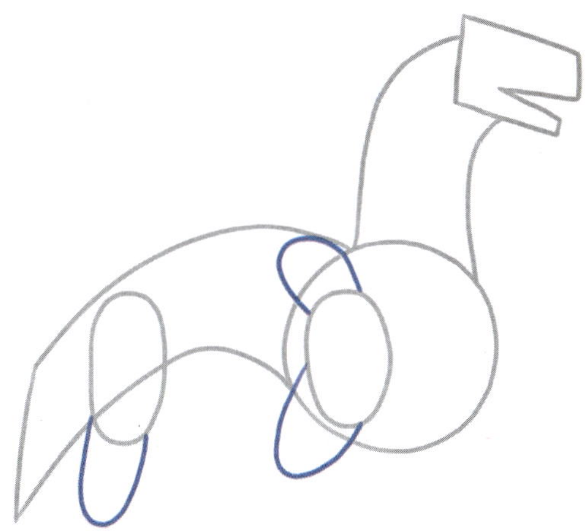

7 Use a curved line to show the top of Sunny's left arm peeking out from behind her body. Then lightly sketch in the basic shapes in Sunny's wings. Her left wing starts as a triangle at the back of her neck, and her right wing attaches to the tail shape.

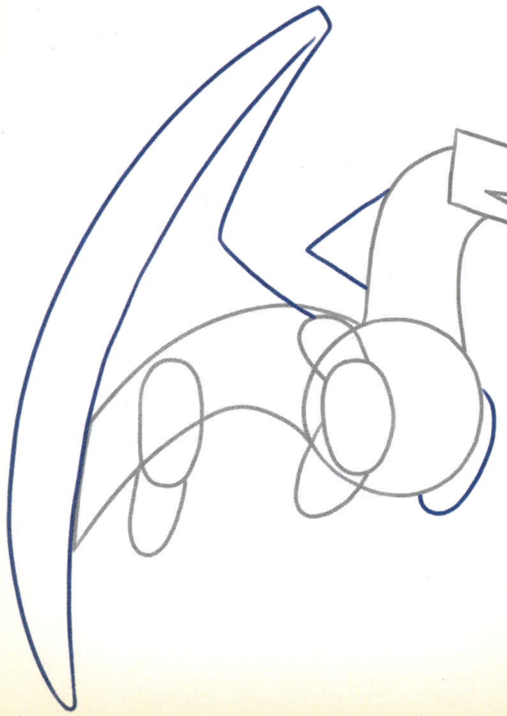

8 Draw a line between the back of her head to the right wing. Then pencil in Sunny's ears and adjust the shape of her face. When you are ready, finish adding the basic shapes of the legs and arms. Notice that her left foot sits higher than her right foot.

9 Draw the tip of Sunny's tail. Do you see the way it curls behind her right wing? Her left ear and the bottom tip of her left wing peek out in a similar way. Finish up by drawing the T-bone shapes in her wings.

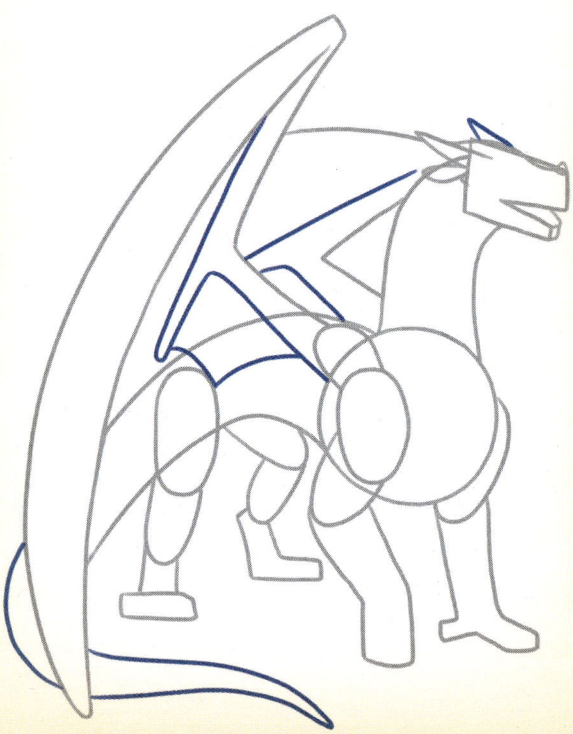

10 Are the lines in this drawing getting confusing? Take a minute to erase the red lines and adjust the others. Is the outline of Sunny's body clearer? Do her arms and legs look more realistic?

11 Time for details! Start drawing the talons. Then sketch in the facial features starting with the eye. Pay attention to the shape of Sunny's snout and the squiggly edge inside her mouth.

12 SandWings have a ridge that runs along their spine. Draw it using an uneven line. Then adjust the outlines of Sunny's back legs and take on those talons. Notice the way the talons on her right foot sit inside the rectangle you drew back in step 8.

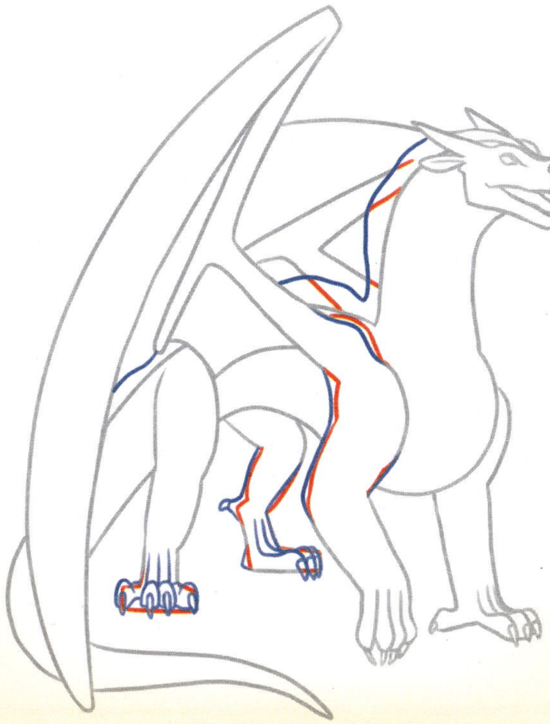

13 Draw the guidelines that will help you place the scales and wing bones in the next step. Then add details like the spike at the end of her wing and sharp teeth inside her mouth.

14 Scale up! Draw the heat-radiating scales that cover Sunny's body. Then color her in with the brightest golden yellow you can find. Her eyes are gray green, and her heart is solid gold!

STARFLIGHT

Starflight has always loved to read and learn, but he never really felt brave — until he had to face his fears and save his friends. Starflight is resting in this pose, which makes it different from the other drawings in this book. Does that sound challenging? Starflight faced his fears, and you can, too! Take it one step at a time.

1 Draw a circle in the lower right-hand corner of your paper for the body. Leave enough space around it to draw more shapes.

2 Starflight is in a resting pose, so the basic shape of the head sits right on top of the body. The head should face left. Draw it the same way you drew Sunny's head.

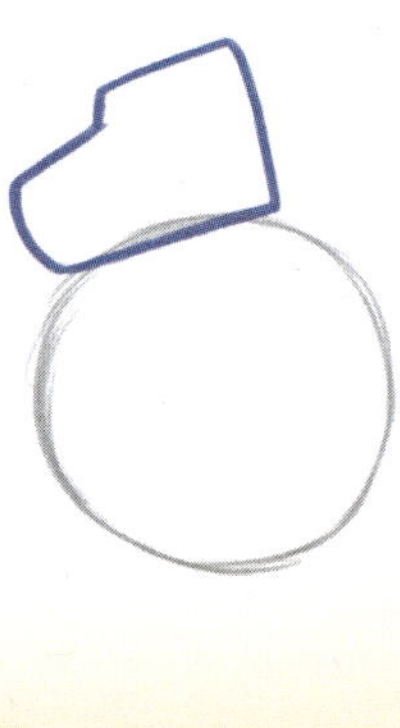

3 Starting at the top right of the head, draw a curved line that ends on top of the body circle. Then draw a smaller line by the jaw to show where the neck creases.

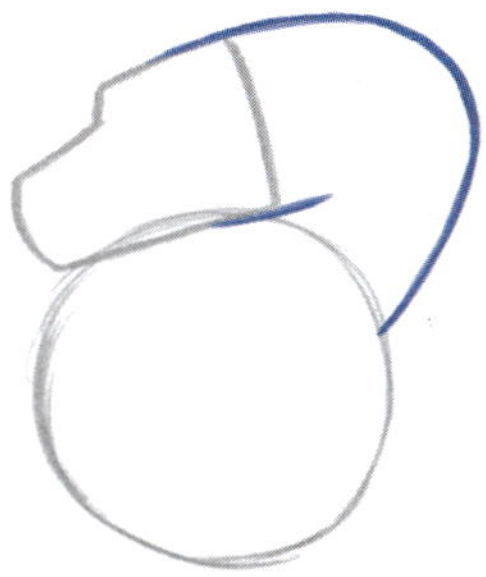

4 Draw two shapes like flippers for the upper arms. Then sketch a squiggly line for the mouth.

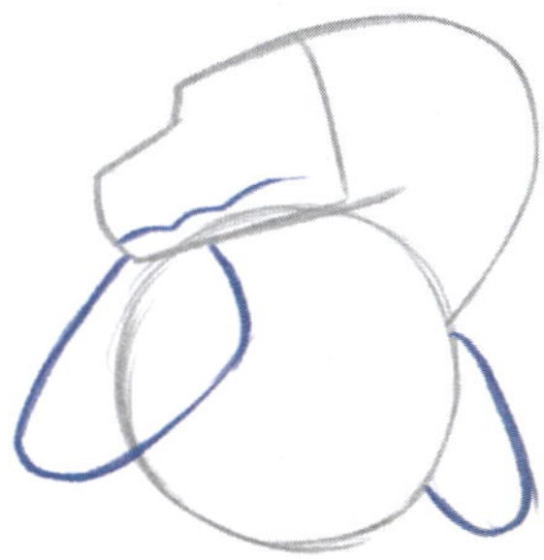

5 Now draw the basic shapes of the forearms and hands.

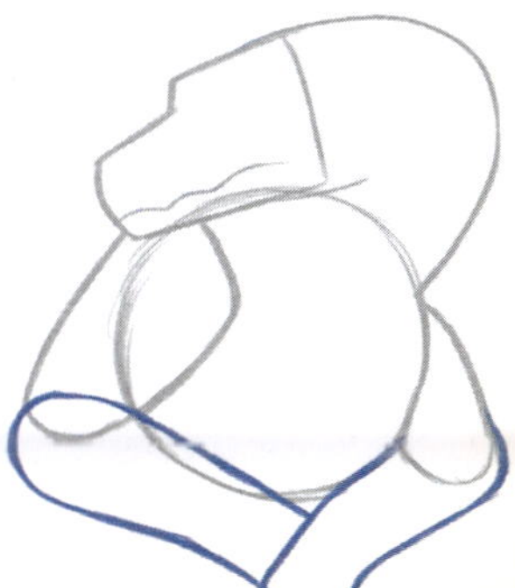

6 Draw Starflight's long, curved tail. The top line of the tail starts at his snout, and the bottom line starts above the elbow.

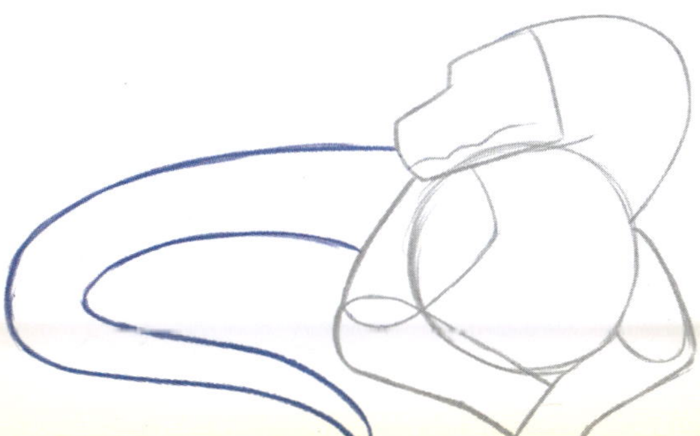

7 Draw a long, curved line for the left wing that starts at the elbow and sweeps up behind the neck. Then draw a right angle for the right wing. This one starts where the nose meets the tail and ends inside the curve of the tail.

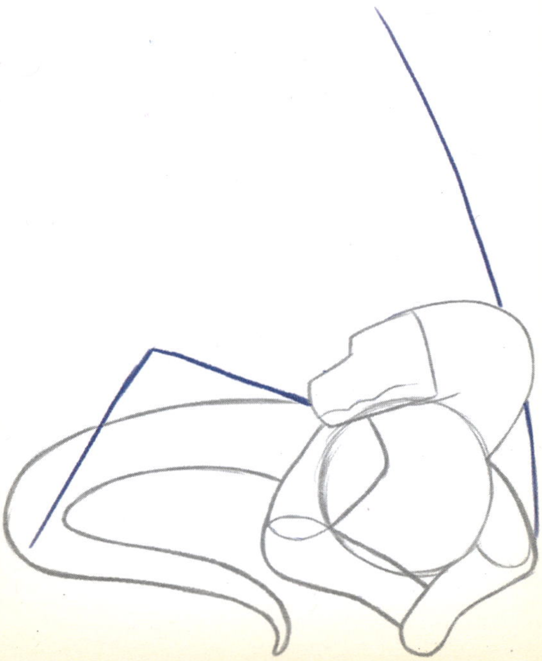

8 Draw the outer curves of the wings. The top edges are scalloped like bat wings. Now sketch the basic shapes of the back leg. Starflight is lying down, so his ankle and leg peek out from under his wing.

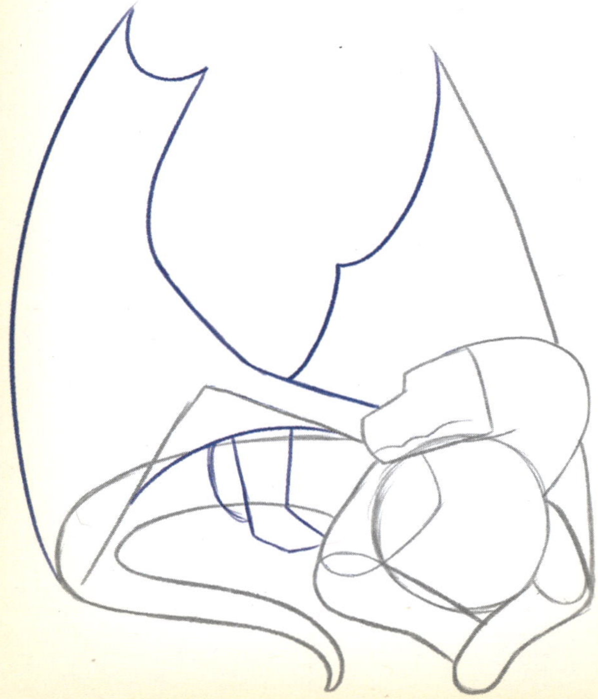

9 Draw the horns at the back of Starflight's head along with his ear and eye. Then move on to the bones and talons on the wings. Use straight lines and triangular shapes for the bones. Pay attention to the way they connect to the lines you've already drawn.

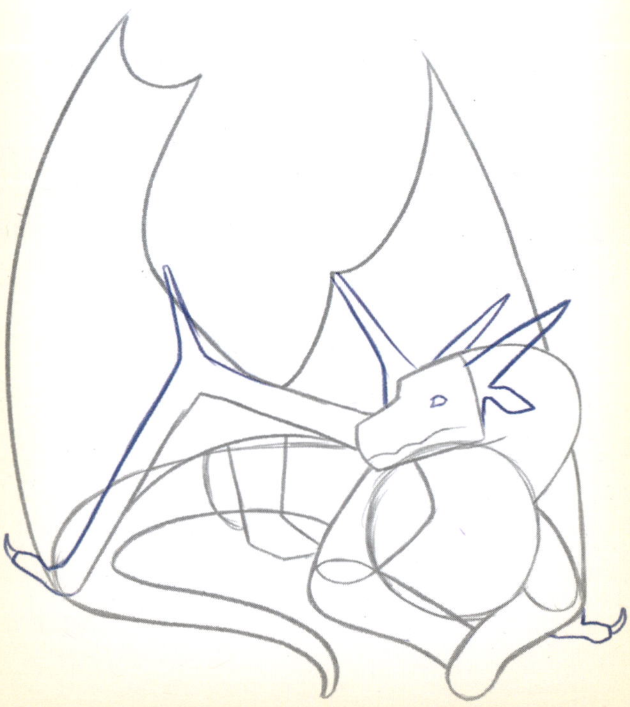

10 Delete the red lines. Then take a good look at your drawing. Does the right wing look like it sits in front of the tail? Does the right arm rest in front of the body? It's amazing how erasing a few lines can give a drawing so much dimension!

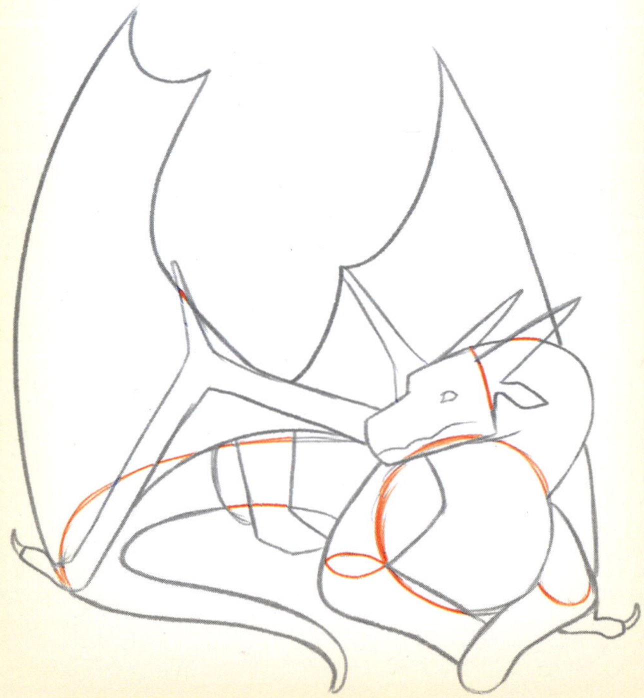

11 Add details to the face and ear. Then use curved lines to show the bends in the arm and neck. If the lines of the snout and brow feel too intimidating, trace them on scrap paper before you begin. Or flip back to the tips on drawing faces on page 5.

12 Use long, slightly curved lines to add segments to the wings. Draw a "U" shape between each of these lines on the top edges of the wings. This is what gives them a scalloped edge. Then tack on some talons.

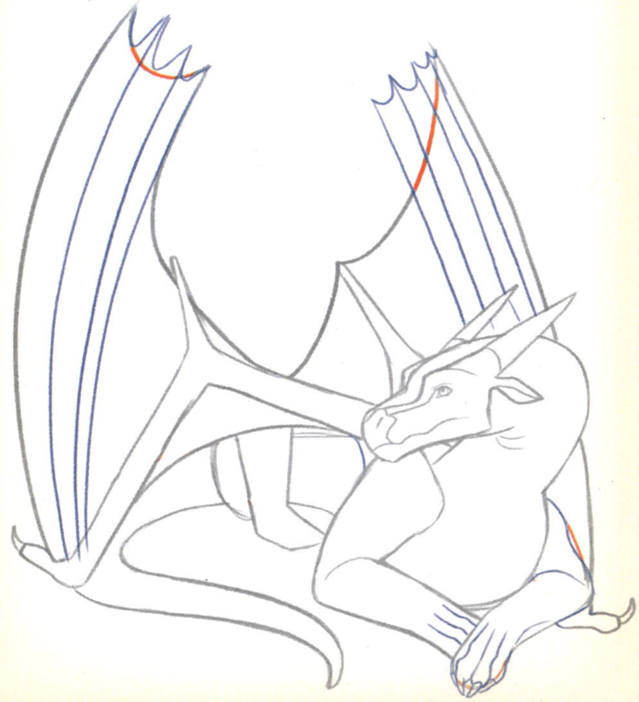

13 Add spikes to Starflight's neck and tail. Then add more talons to the toes. Use curved lines on the tail, chest, and neck to make them look three-dimensional. Reshape any edges that don't feel quite right.

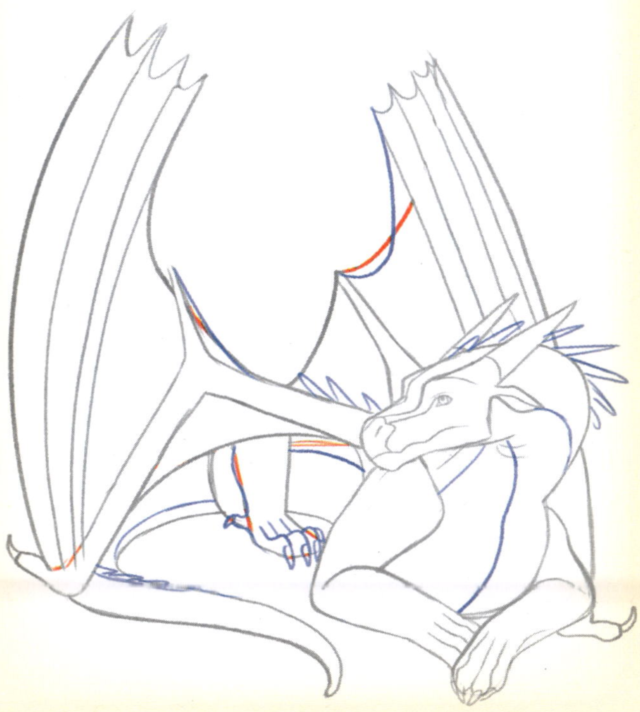

14 Reshape each of the segments in the wing until they look like long, bony fingers. Then draw a talon at the end of each one. Starflight's scales are the color of midnight, and the silver scales on the underside of his wings spread outward like water splashing.

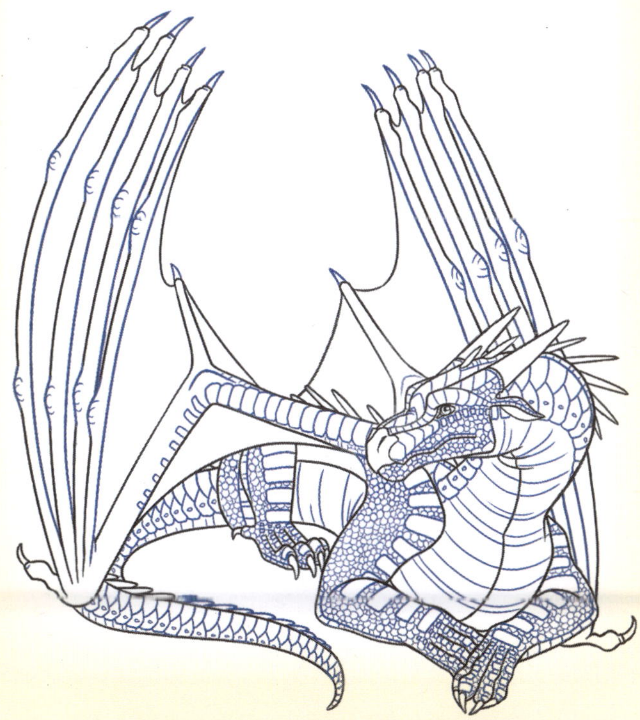

GLORY

For years, Glory was taught that dragons from her tribe were too lazy to accomplish much. Then Glory led a rescue mission into NightWing territory *and* competed to become the queen of the RainWings *and* the NightWings. Glory never lets anyone else tell her what she's good at, and neither should you! Want to get better at drawing? Stick with it!

1 Start with a circle for the body.

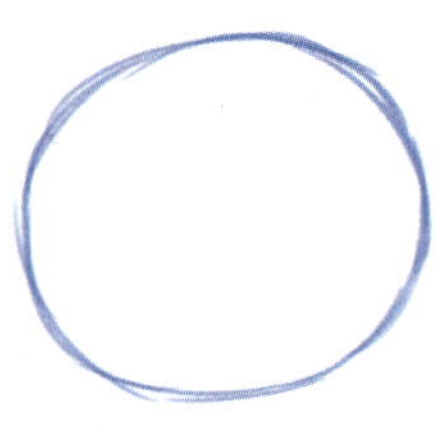

2 Draw a starter shape for the head. Use the right angle on the right side and the sideways "V" on the left to help you. The final shape should look like it's about to eat the body. Notice how much space there is between these shapes.

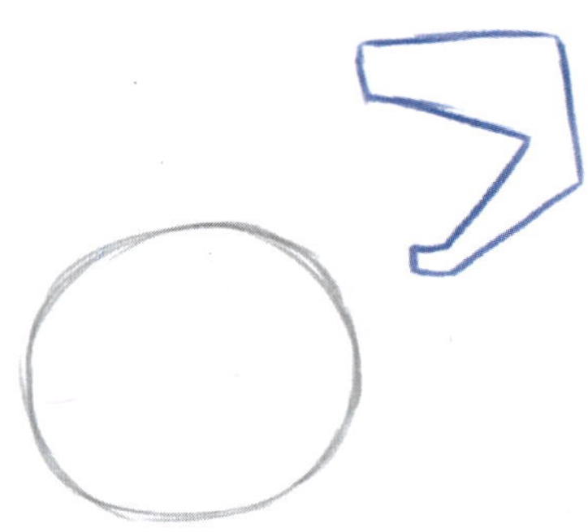

3 Connect the head to the body with two curved lines for the neck. Then draw another "V" shape inside the mouth to make it three-dimensional. Is Glory looking back over her shoulder? She'd better be, with Scarlet on her tail!

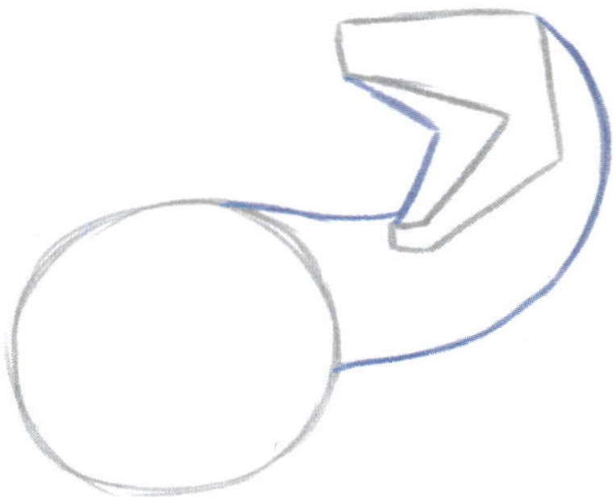

4 Draw a long, curved line for Glory's tail. It has a curlicue at the tip, just like the one you drew for Kinkajou. Notice where the tail connects to the body circle.

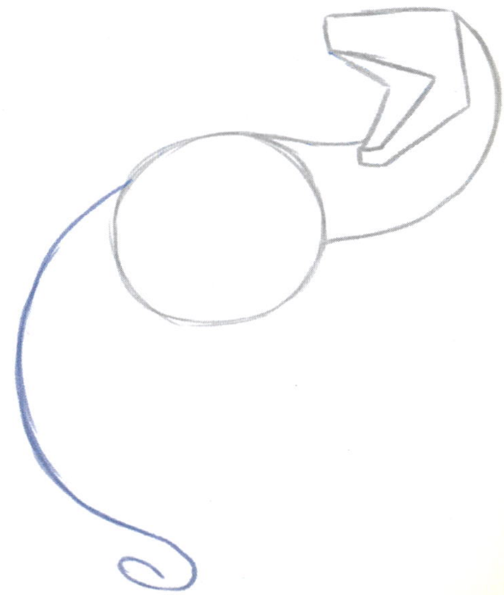

5 Widen the tail, then use a second curved line to give the tail form.

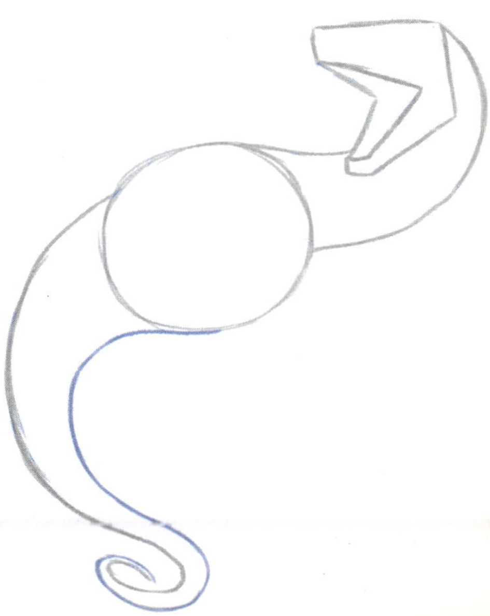

6 Set up the basic shapes of the right arm and leg. Arms and legs usually start with clusters or groups of shapes. The shapes for the leg — two ovals and a teardrop — sit inside the tail. The starter shapes for the arm rest inside the circle you drew for the body.

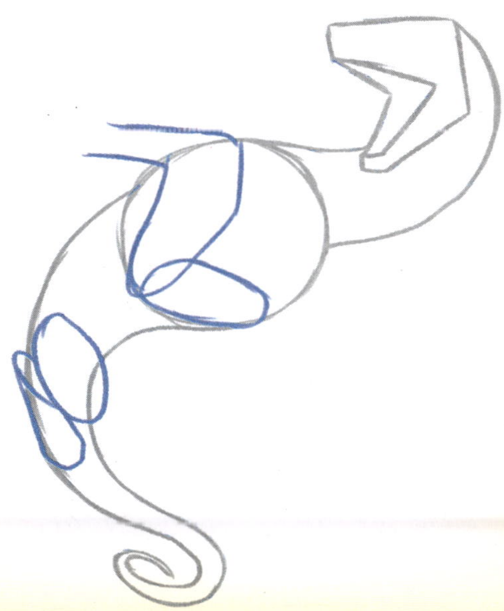

7 Keep building onto the shapes you've drawn for the arms and legs. Take it step-by-step and shape by shape. Then draw the basic shape of the wing. Don't forget to draw the ear and horn!

8 Sketch in Glory's left wing. Use scalloped lines at the bottom just like you did for her friends. Then add a talon to the top of her right wing, the colorful flap behind her ear, and the basic shape of her eye.

9 Whew! You're making progress! Erase the red lines and examine your drawing. Does anything need to be redrawn or erased before you start adding details to the face?

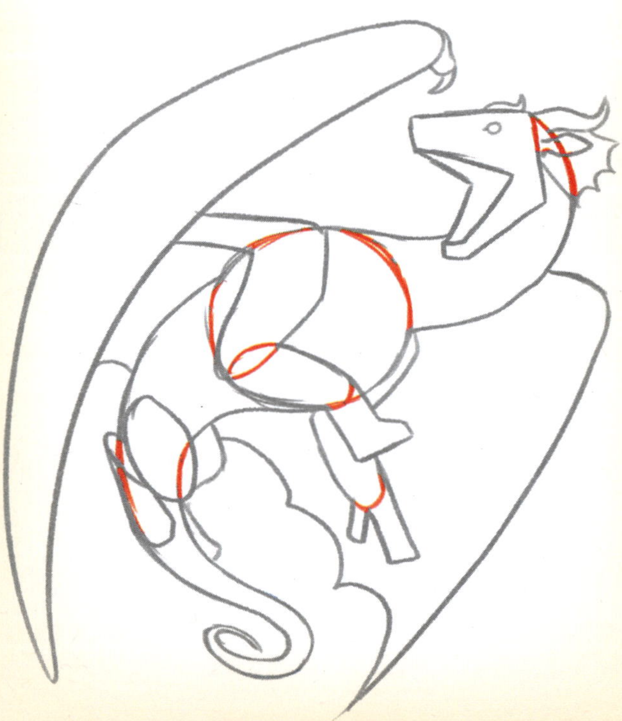

10 Add nostrils and reshape the outlines of Glory's face to make it look realistic. Keep erasing old guidelines as you go along. Does the outline of Glory's body look a little more dragonlike? You're on the right track!

11 Like most other dragon tribes, RainWings have forked tongues and sharp fangs. And this pose gives you a great view! Draw those details, and then tackle the talons on her right foot. Use the starter shapes you drew in step 7 to help position each toe.

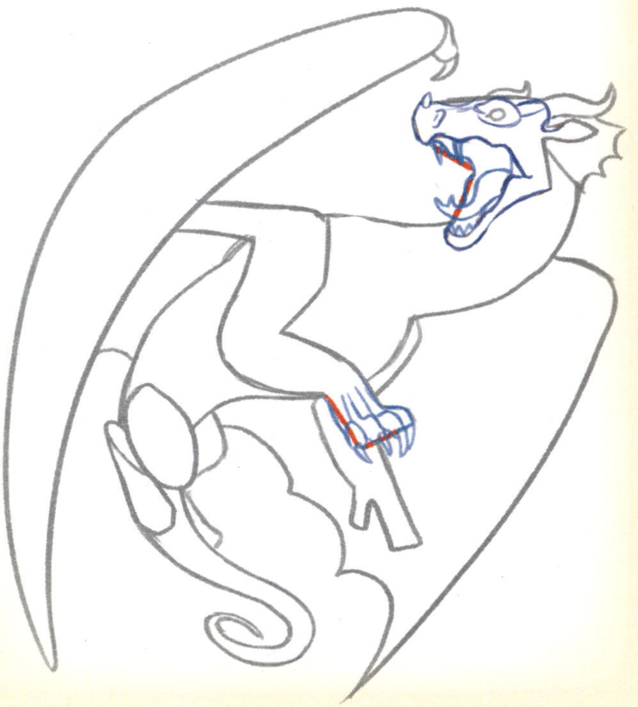

12 Finish up the talons and continue to refine the shape of the arms and legs. Take a closer look at that left hand. The top line of each talon runs parallel to the sides of the starter shape, and the curves at the bottom rest on the same horizontal line.

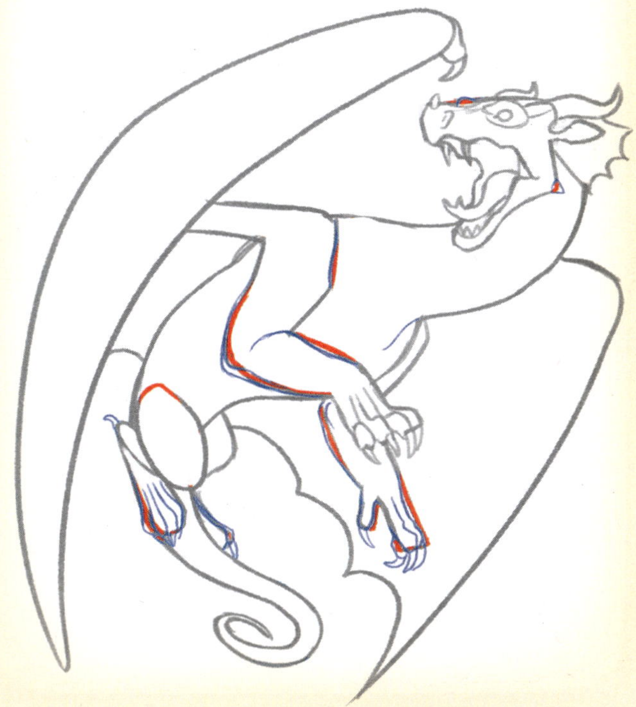

13 Curved lines add detail and depth. Use them to set off the segments in Glory's ruff and wings. Use them on her neck and body to separate her scales from her softer underbelly. Finish off this step by adding spines to her back.

14 Finish up the details in Glory's scales, face, and mouth. Then get ready to add color! RainWing scales change color depending on their mood. What mood do you think Glory is in?

SCARLET

This former SkyWing queen thrives on vengeance and rage. And she *loves* coming up with new strategies for terrifying dragons! What strategies will you use to draw this ruthless royal? What color paper will you use to make her red-orange scales pop? How will you break down the basic shapes? The steps in this book are suggestions. Feel free to make your own plan!

1 Start with a large circle for the body. Then draw a rectangular head with a triangular mouth. Draw a small circle in the air in front of the mouth. Does it look like the head is about to eat the smaller circle? Even Scarlet's starter shapes are ruthless!

2 Scarlet is looking back in this pose, so her neck curves dramatically. Draw the top curve of the neck first. It runs from the nose to the body circle. The bottom curve of the neck runs from the jaw to the bottom of the body circle. Finish with a tiny line between the middle of her neck and the body. The tail gets attached to the smaller circle.

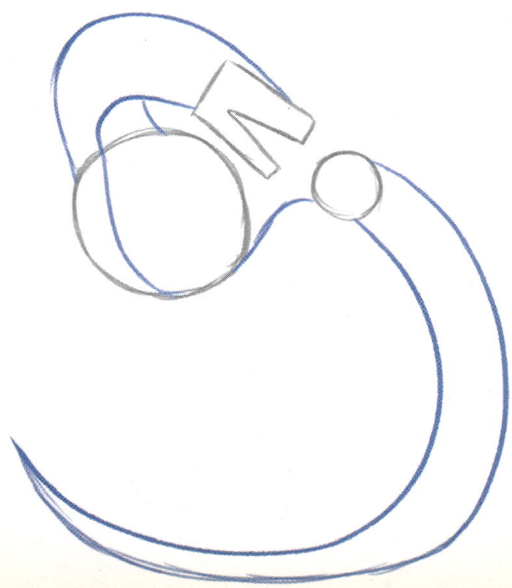

3 Draw the boxy shape of Scarlet's right wing behind the curve of her neck. Then draw the starter shapes for her arms. The upper arms have similar winglike shapes.

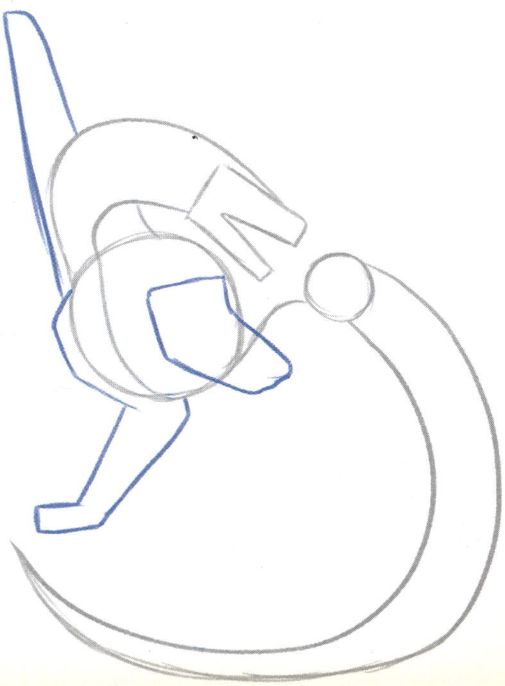

4 Draw the bottom of her right arm. Then attach two wavy horns and an ear to the back of her head. Now focus on the left wing. See where it attaches to the body with two short, straight lines? Use sweeping curves for the rest of the wing.

5 Draw two lines between the jaw and upper arm and one inside the mouth. Then draw a circle for her eye. Attach the basic shapes of Scarlet's left leg to the small circle you drew in step 1. The right leg is marked by a line behind her left elbow and a small box behind her left arm.

6 Scarlet has no problem getting rid of anything — or any*one* — she decides is unnecessary. Erase the lines you don't need. Then calculate your next move!

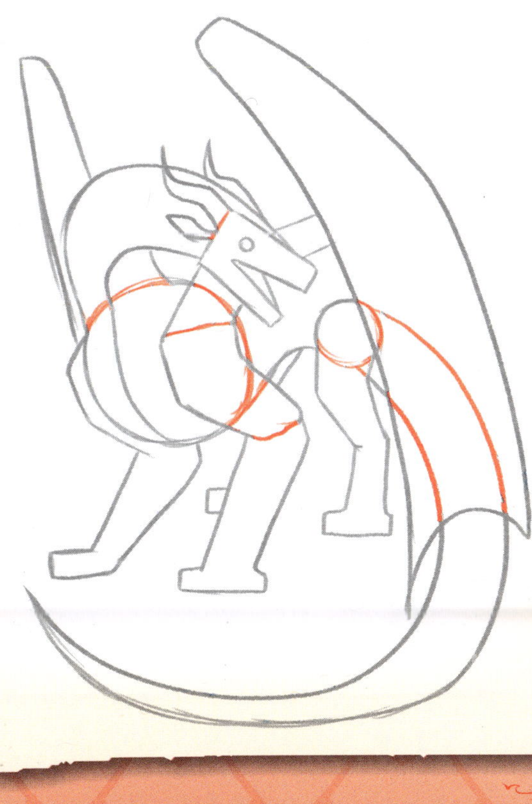

7

The lines in this step will add dimension to your drawing. Pay attention to where each one starts and ends. Then draw the talons on Scarlet's right foot. Notice how one talon sits up on her ankle.

8

Dastardly details! The details in her face work together to make Scarlet's expression as maniacal as her personality. The dot of her pupil, the downturned edge of her wide-open mouth, the angles of her brow, and her triangular snout all give her a wild, unpredictable look!

9

Draw three short lines around her eye, small sharp teeth, and a line inside the mouth for her tongue. Add detail lines at her elbows and talons on her left foot. Then draw a circular line around her neck for her diamond-and-gold circlet.

10

Draw the straight and craggy edges of her wing bones. Don't forget the scalloped edge of her batlike wing.

11 Keep building up the details! Draw the talon on top of her right wing. Then draw a curved line inside her tail, starting near the tip. Notice that it starts on the inner edge and ends on the outer edge.

12 Refine the outlines as you go along. Pay particular attention to her left leg. How can you reshape the outline to make it feel more organic, less boxy, and more like a dragon leg? Then draw in some talons using the starter shapes as a guide.

13 Deep-dive into details! Draw the spikes that run along Scarlet's spine, the claw on her elbow, and the talons on her right toe. Then draw some detail lines inside her right wing.

14 What finishing touches can you add to make your drawing of Scarlet look as fierce as the real deal? Her dark orange scales and yellow eyes glow like flames, and smoke billows from her nostrils. The whole look is killer-queen chic!

DARKSTALKER

This NightWing-IceWing was one of the most powerful dragons ever to hatch in Pyrrhia. He grew to be three times the size of most dragons and had both animus and prophetic powers — along with the ability to read minds! Here's a prophecy for you: You'll have great drawing success with Darkstalker! Before you get started, try using an extra-long pencil.

1 Draw a circle. Then draw two short, straight lines coming out of it. The top line should lean to the right. This will be the neck. Draw a small circle at the end of each guideline.

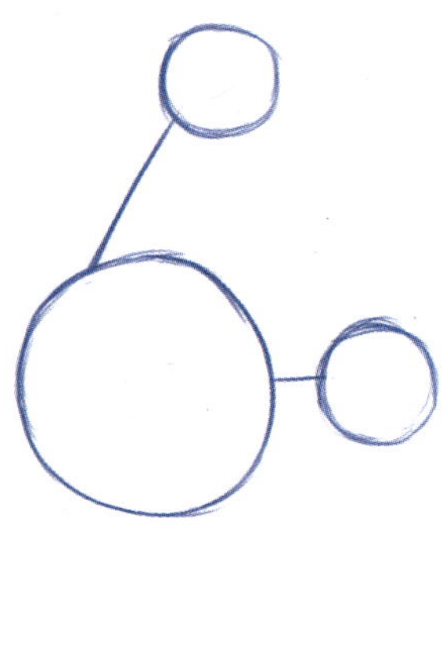

2 Starting at the base of the head, draw a long, sinewy line that curves down on the left side of the neck, through the body, across the second small circle, and drops into a long tail that loops back around at the tip.

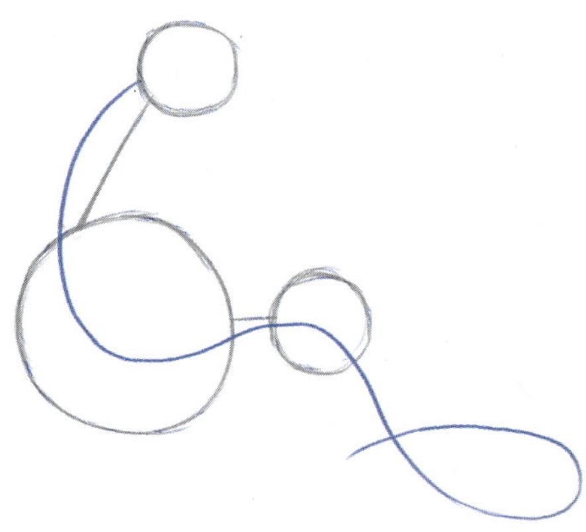

3 Use curved lines to connect the body circle and the backside circle.

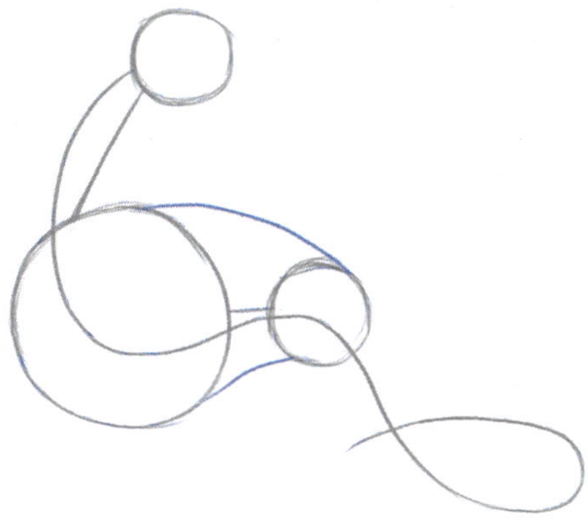

4 The lines that connect the head and body swoop around to the left. See how long the line on the left is compared to the line on the right side?

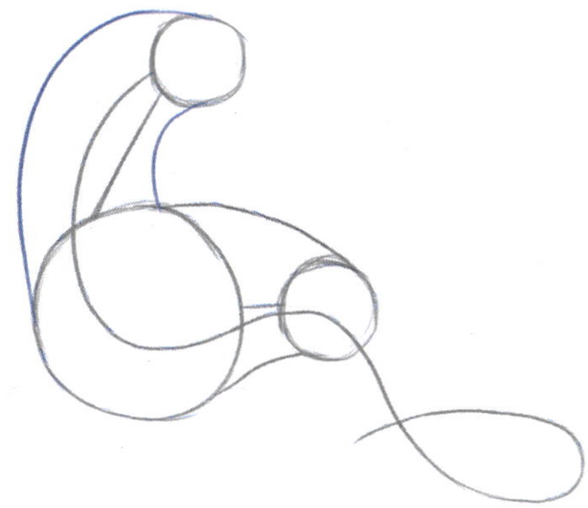

5 Tail time! The tail is made up of three separate lines. The bottom curve starts at the bottom of the lower circle. The top curve starts at the top of the lower circle. They both end when they reach the guideline you drew in step 2. To make the tail look three-dimensional, draw a small curve on the inner edge.

6 Build the shapes for Darkstalker's left arm and leg as if you're building a robot. Each shape connects to the next, one by one. Each thigh is an oval. The front knee is a circle. What shapes and lines do you see in the lower legs and feet?

7 The right arm and leg are made up of the same basic shapes as the left arm and leg, except they are partially hidden by the body. The right back leg is a mirror image of the left back leg!

8 For Darkstalker's right wing bone, draw a long, skinny rectangle at the base of the neck. On his left, draw a rectangle with a triangle at the top. Then draw a straight line from the base of the triangle to the body circle and connect it to the thigh circle with a short, curved line.

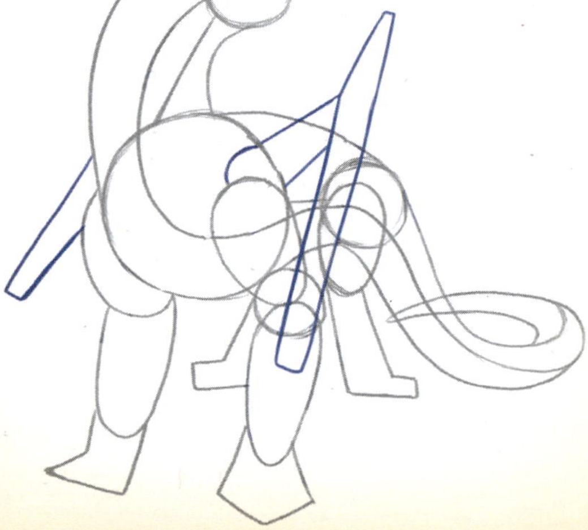

9 Use long, sweeping lines to block in the general outline of the wings. Notice where each line connects to the body.

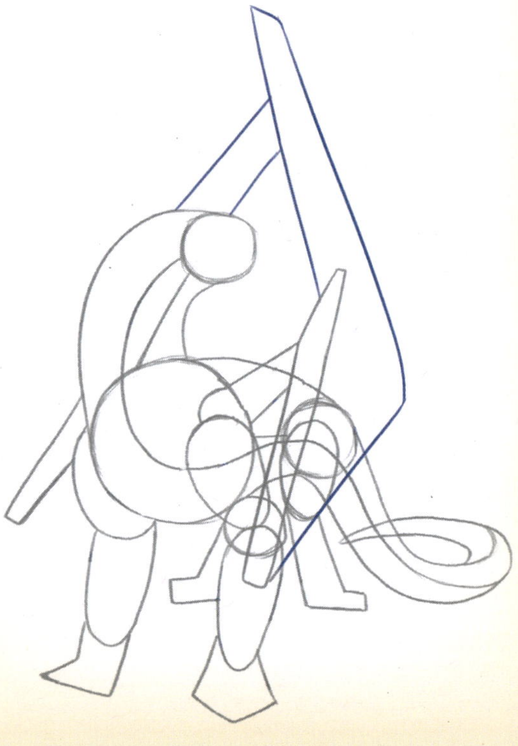

10 Block in the basic shape of the head. Then add two quick lines that look like antennae. Bumblebee's and Kinkajou's heads were angled up to show off their bright personalities. This NightWing's head tilts down to reflect a much darker state.

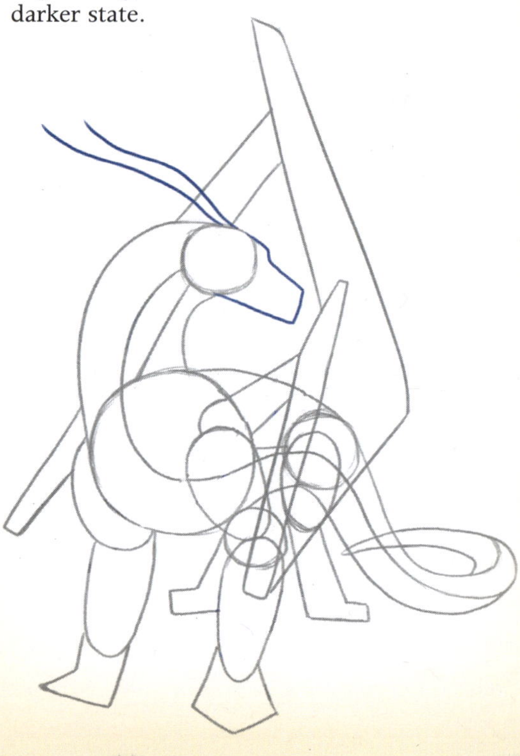

11 Using the antennae you drew in step 10 as a guide, draw the bottom of Darkstalker's twisted horns. Then draw a diamond-shaped ear and a straight guideline for the closed mouth.

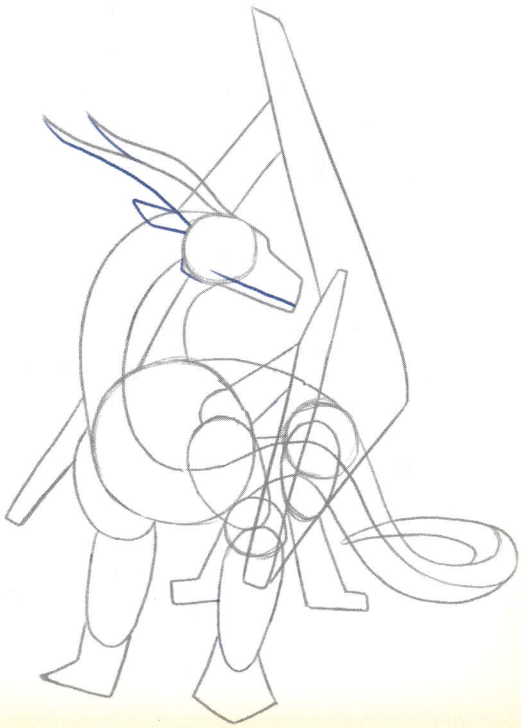

12 Erase any lines you don't need and clean up the outlines. Then double-check the proportions. Finish up by adding details to the ears and face. A squiggly line will give the illusion of sharp teeth. Another curvy line sets off the triangular snout.

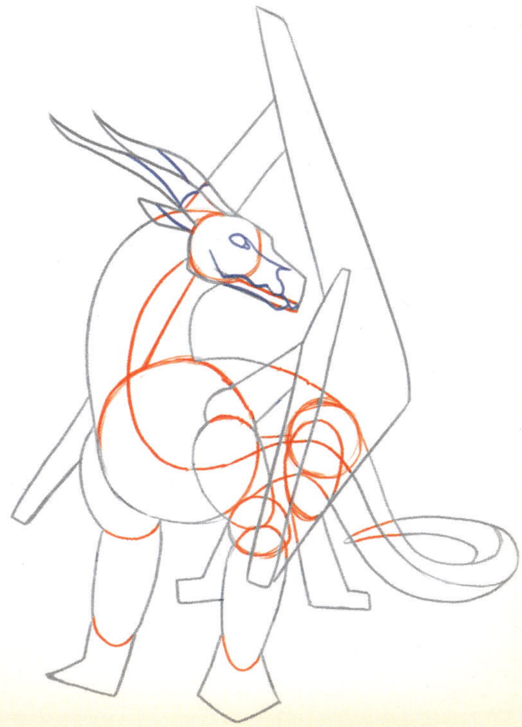

13 Fill in the pupil, leaving a white circle for the devious gleam in Darkstalker's eye. Then sketch in his brooding brows and add a curved guideline to the neck. It starts at the throat.

14 Terrifying talons! Use this step to make the legs more lifelike by rounding out their edges. Then use the basic shapes of the feet to help you decide where to draw each talon.

15

Top off each wing with its own terrible talon. Then focus on the back talons. They start with basic bumps/curves — each one gets its own upside-down teardrop.

16

Loosen up your arm before drawing the long, sweeping lines that will become Darkstalker's wing bones. Practice moving your whole arm as you draw — not just your wrist — to keep your lines light and loose.

17

Add feather-like shapes to the back of the neck and along the spine. Then take a closer look at the wings. Notice that each long, curved bone has a bump-out for an elbow and a talon at the tip.

18

Stand back and take a good look at your drawing. Do you want to add the silver teardrop scales at the corner of Darkstalker's eyes? Talons on the back wings? Grab your darkest blue and black markers to make his scales match the night sky.

PERIL

Peril was raised to be Queen Scarlet's champion in the arena, fighting and defeating everyone she faced. But once she met Clay — the only dragon whose scales don't burn at her touch — Peril realized making friends might be more fun than fighting. Which friends will you invite to draw with you?

1 Start with a jelly bean shape for the body that is wider on the top than on the bottom. Draw a small circle above the jelly bean and a little to the right. Connect the circle to the body with a line that curves in the middle.

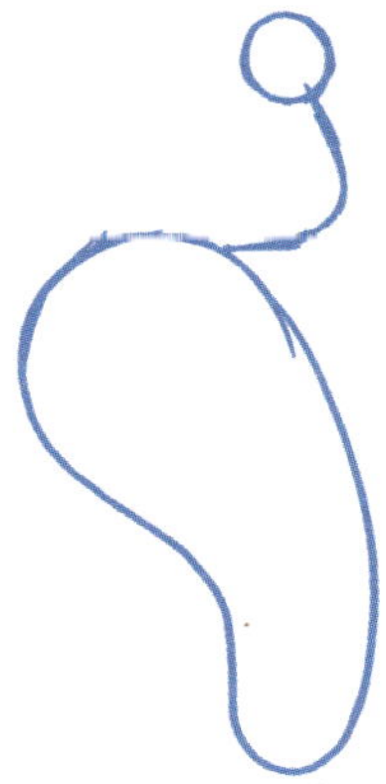

2 Draw a long, curved line for the tail. Then use two curved lines to add thickness to the neck. Next, draw the rectangular shapes of the snout and jaw just like you did for Bumblebee and Kinkajou.

3 Draw a second curved line starting at the back of the jelly bean to widen the tail. Make sure the lines meet at the tip. Sketch in a group of ovals to set up the arms. Then attach the basic shapes of the hands.

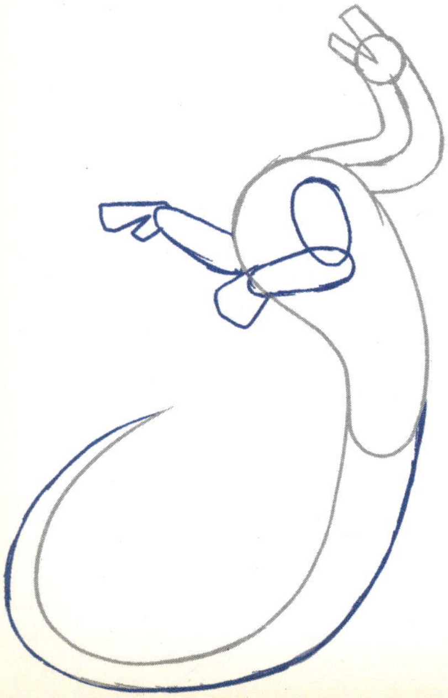

4 Take the left leg step-by-step. Start by drawing an oval on an angle. This is the thigh. Then draw a curve below the oval for the shin. Attach a teardrop shape to the shin. Next, draw a curved line that peeks out from behind the tail. This is the right thigh and knee. Now draw a peekaboo rectangle for the right foot.

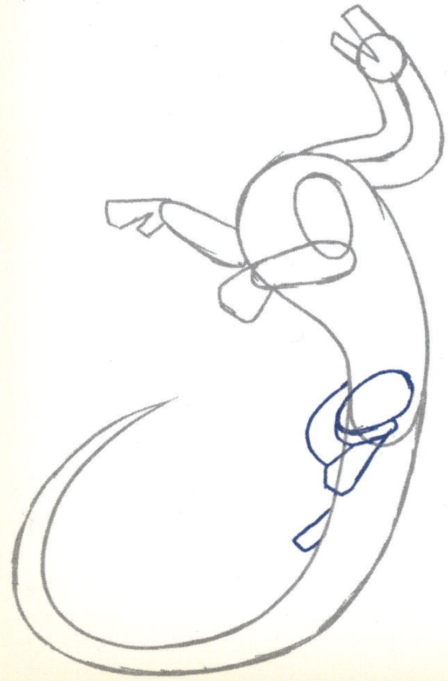

5 Attach a long, skinny oval to the top of the left shoulder. This will be a wing bone. Do you see the tip of the right wing bone peeking out from behind the body? Draw that, too. Then use a bent line like a "V" to set up the right wing.

6 Draw the outlines of the wings using long, sweeping curves. Then draw Peril's curvy horn and the outline of her eye. This SkyWing is ready to breathe fire, so draw an angled line inside her mouth to make it look three-dimensional.

7 See the red lines in the book? Erase them on your drawing. Is it easier to see the way Peril's left knee bends toward you? Once the lines are where you want them, draw in Peril's facial features.

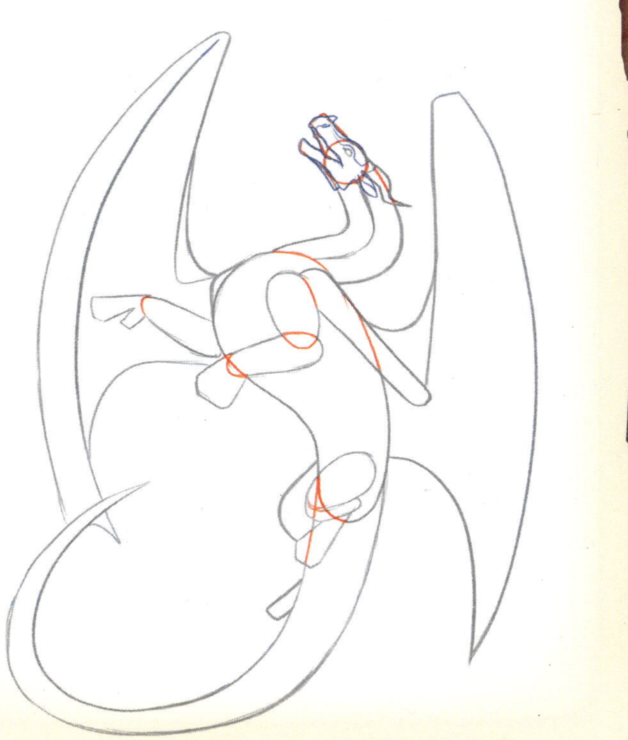

8 Draw the wing bone in her left wing. Then start drawing in Peril's terrible tearing talons. Continue to refine the shape of the arms.

9 Draw two curved lines in the tail to make it look more three-dimensional. They'll also help you place the scales in the next step. Then draw the segments of the wings just like you did for Starflight. Don't forget the talons on top of her wings.

10 Clean up your outlines and get ready to color. Peril has unusually bright metallic-orange firescales that are so hot they actually give off heat — making her look like she's burning from the inside!

MOONWATCHER

As a NightWing who can hear other dragons' thoughts, it can be hard for Moonwatcher to concentrate. But she has a trick. She imagines putting each voice inside a raindrop and letting it fall away. Sometimes our own inner voice tells us a drawing is too hard. Tuck that voice inside a raindrop and let it go. You've got this!

1 Start by drawing a circle for this NightWing's body.

2 Draw the outline of her head above the circle and off to the left.

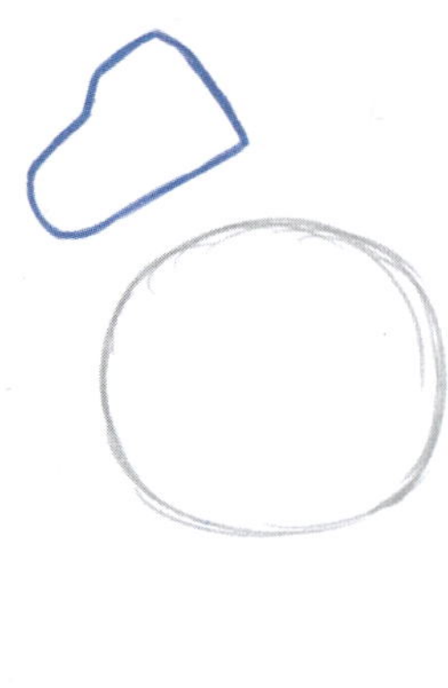

3 Connect the head to the body with two curved lines.

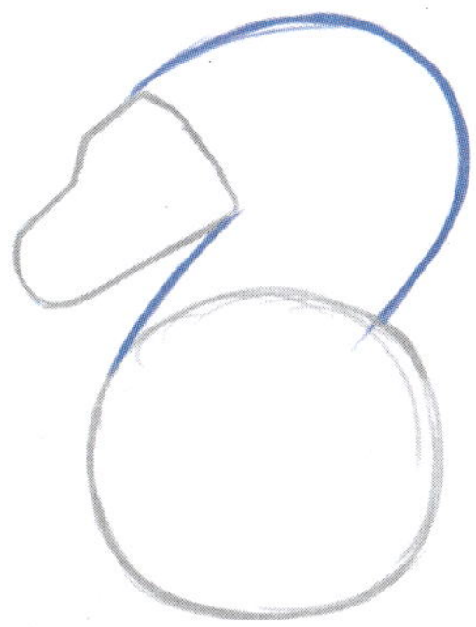

4 Use ovals to sketch the basic shapes of Moon's front legs. The top circle will be her shoulder. Starting at the shoulder circle, draw a guideline for the front wing. It should look like a zigzag that runs off the bottom edge of the paper.

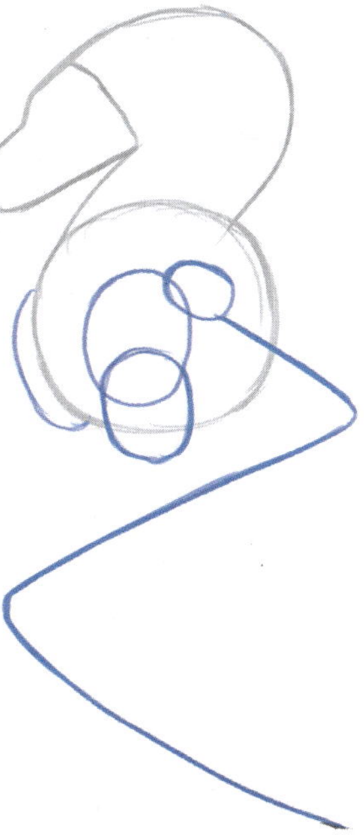

5 Expand the wing by drawing the wing bone and scalloped edge. In this drawing, the wing is so big and close to you, it should pop right off the page.

6 Continue drawing the basic shapes of the forearm and hands. The shape that looks like a wrist cuff will become her right hand. Then build up the wings. Look at the top of the left wing. Three curved lines will close off that shape. Another three lines at the front of the chest will form the top of the right wing.

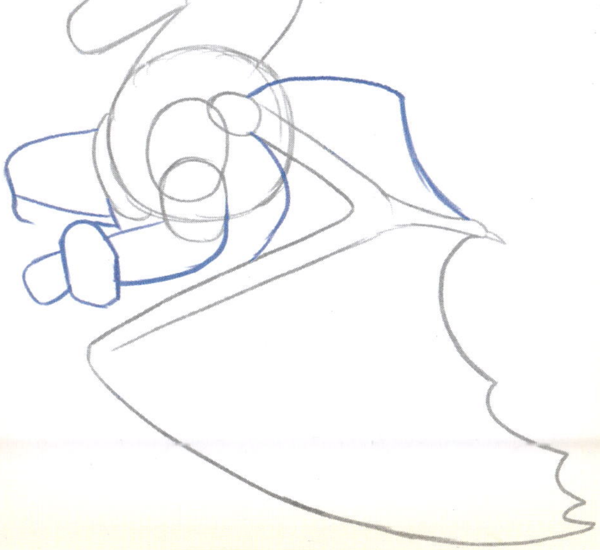

7 Draw a big curve from the back of Moon's neck to the middle of her wing. This will be the back of the body. Then draw the talons on her wings. Focus on the lines and shapes at the front of the body. Those curves form the tip of the tail.

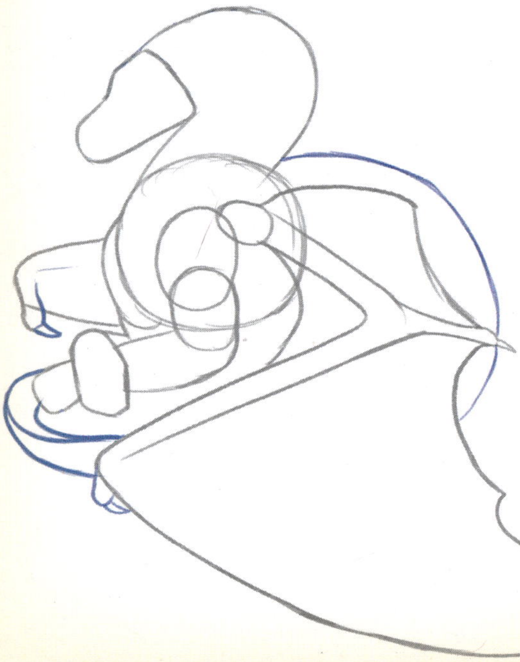

8 Draw Moon's straight NightWing horns and diamond-shaped ear. Then add a line for her mouth and curved lines for the snout and brow. Next, erase the red lines and check the proportions. Is there anything else you'd like to erase or redraw?

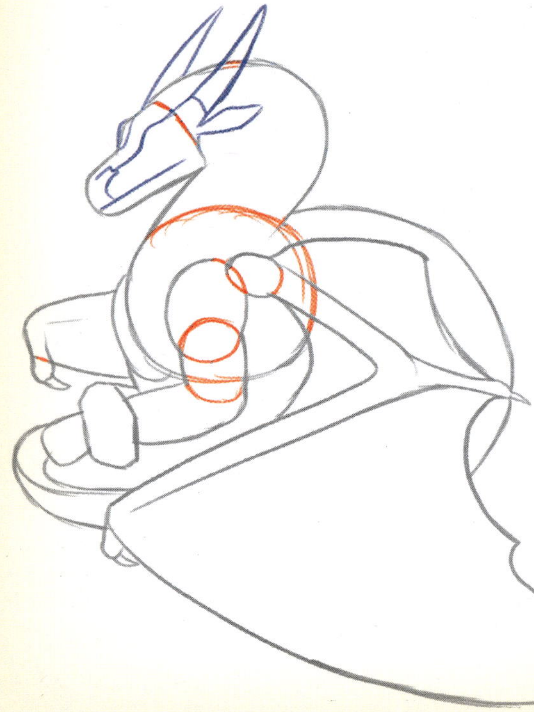

9 Congrats! You've got the basics of the body down, and it's time to add details! Draw the outline of the eye and two squiggles on the mouth line. Then draw four straight lines on the wing to show where it folds. Don't forget the talons on the right hand.

10 Only a few NightWings have a teardrop shape next to their eyes — and Moon is one of them! Draw it now. Then reshape the edges of the snout and upper arm. Add a short, curved line where the arm bends.

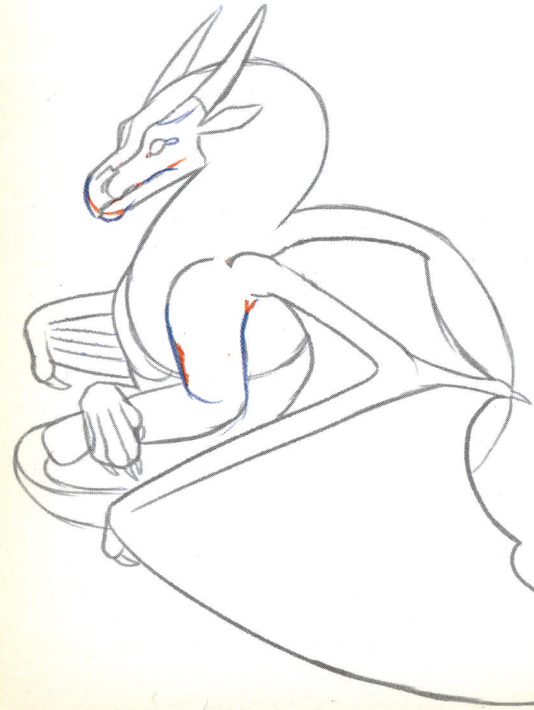

11 Draw a curved line from the back of Moon's head to her shoulder. It should run parallel to the other lines you drew for the neck. Then add more details to the face and ear.

12 Start adding sharp spines to the back of Moon's neck. Then finish up the talons on her left hand.

13 Draw more spikes along her back. Draw three sweeping lines to show the segments of the wings.

14 Finalize your outlines and draw Moonwatcher's protective scales. Then get ready to add color! If Moon could hear your thoughts, what would she know about you?

QIBLI

As an Outclaw and advisor to Queen Thorn, Qibli has always had to be on high alert. When he steps into a new situation, he sizes it up and looks for any potential pitfalls. Want to size up this drawing before you begin? Try flipping to step 14 and reading the steps backward to get a feel for the way all the lines and shapes connect before you begin!

1 Start with a circle for the body.

2 Draw a rectangle on an angle for the head. Leave enough space between the two shapes for the neck.

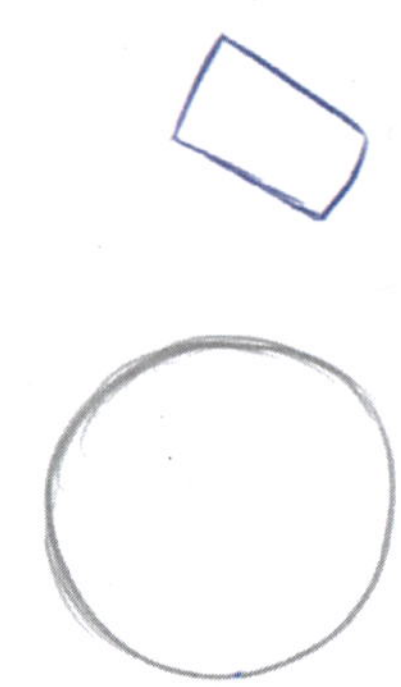

3 Draw two curved lines for Qibli's neck.

4 Use long ovals for the upper arms. If it helps, you can draw the whole oval for Qibli's left arm and erase the part that's hidden behind his body.

5 Attach the basic shapes of the forearm and hand to the oval you drew in step 4. Then draw a short, curved line coming out from the elbow. Then add a long, curved line to set up the tail. The line starts at the wrist and ends out in front of the body.

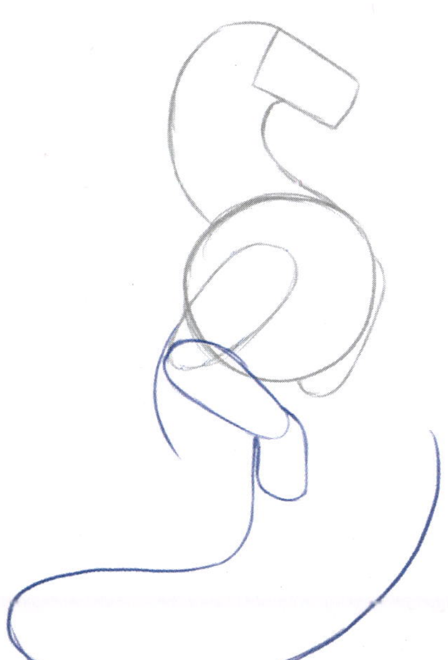

6 Remember that curve you drew in step 5? Draw an angled oval at the end of it for the leg. Then draw the basic shape of the foot below it.

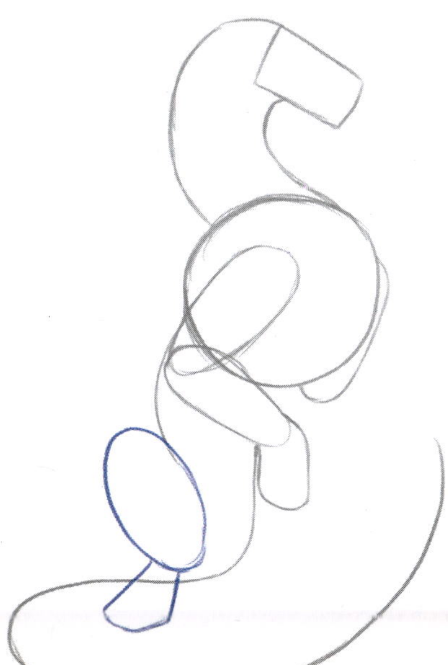

7 Draw a curve inside the leg oval. Then finish the tail by drawing a curved line parallel to the tail line you drew in step 5. To add the SandWing stinger, extend a line out from the tip of the tail. Then draw a curve on the left side like a backward letter "D."

8 Draw Qibli's wings! His left wing attaches at the front of the chest circle. Now draw the long cylinder and shoe shape that make up Qibli's left leg. Finally, draw a curve above the rectangle for the forehead and attach two pointy horns.

9 Draw the facial features and refine the shape of the snout. Add a curved fin at the back of his neck and sketch in the right arm. Pencil in Qibli's hind foot and start adding structure to the wings using both curved and straight lines.

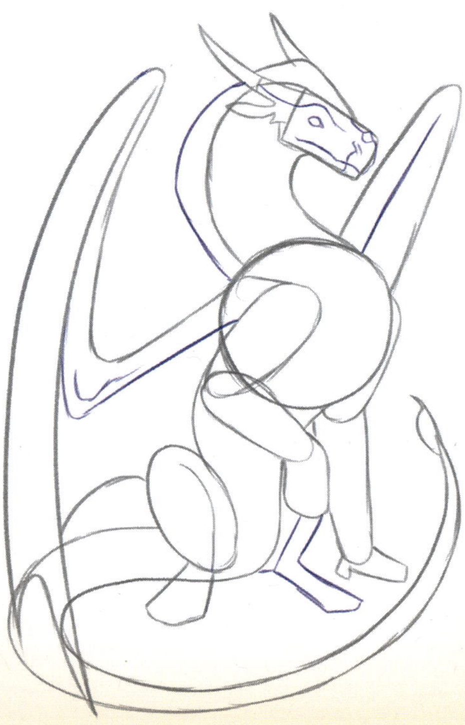

10 Size him up! Is Qibli standing tall and proud? Is his head about the same size as his right leg? Once you've double-checked the angles and proportions, erase any guidelines you no longer need. What details do you still need to add?

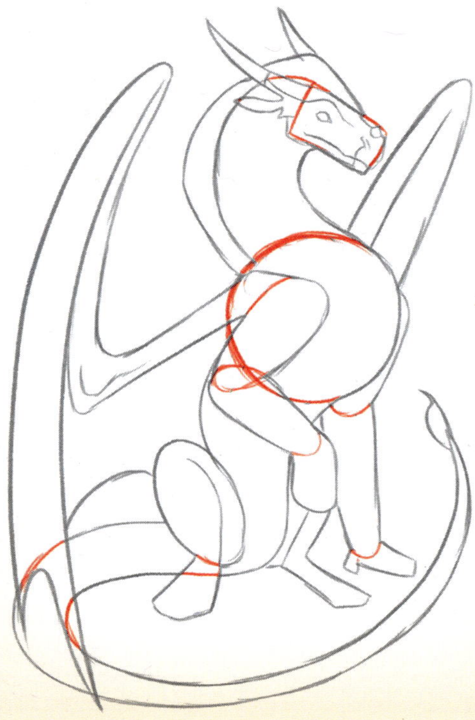

11 Now that you're happy with the outlines and proportions, start adding details like talons on the wings and hands. Then reshape the fin on his neck so the edges ripple like sand dunes.

12 Get even more detailed with the talons on the left hand. Draw a curve on the neck to set off the scales from the underbelly. Then use curved lines to add structure to the wings and an extra sting to the tail.

13 You're almost done! Draw an extra curve on the chest that will help you place the scales in the next step. Draw a ridge on the back of his tail with a short, curved line. Then sketch in an elbow joint on the wing. Don't forget the talons!

14 Are there any details missing? Draw them now! Then color Qibli's scales with pale yellows to match the desert sands. You may even want to trace over the outlines you drew with a thin black marker.

CLIFF

This young SkyWing dragonet is the son of Queen Ruby. He believes he's going to be the best singer in Pyrrhia one day — and also friends with all the dragons. What do you want to be best known for? Is it for a talent, like drawing dragons? Or a personality trait, like the ability to make your friends laugh?

1 Start this drawing with three circles — a big circle for the body and two smaller circles for the head and rear end. Connect the body to the head with a long, curved line for the neck.

2 Draw another curved line to connect the body circle to the rear end circle. Then sketch in the basic shapes of the head and tail. Cliff looks a lot like Bumblebee at this stage.

3 Draw a wavy line for Cliff's mouth. Then focus on the back half of his body. Sketch in the basic shapes of the back legs, then add the tail, and finish up with the wings. Feeling stuck? Trace the parts that feel hard on scrap paper!

4 Sketch in the back wing. Then trace the face! Use scrap paper to practice a few times. All the features on this baby dragon are rounded compared to the full-grown dragons. Don't forget to draw a talon at the spot where the wing bends.

5 Erase any guidelines you don't need anymore and clean up the outlines. When you're ready, draw the bones in the wings and the ridges that run along his spine.

6 Draw scales on the face, details in the eyes, and claws on his tiny talons. Cliff has dark red scales and golden-orange eyes. Ready for an adventure? Draw Cliff soaring through the Sky Kingdom with a new friend!

MINK

This outgoing and creative IceWing princess is the youngest daughter of Queen Glacier. She loves building ice sculptures in the snow and *always* wants to play. Mink can't wait to explore the world beyond the Ice Kingdom. Are you ready to explore more drawing techniques?

1 Start by drawing a large circle for the body and a smaller one for the head. Connect them with two curved lines for the neck. Then add another curve for the hind end.

2 Start to place the legs and wings, just like you've done for previous dragons. What shape is her right wing? Where does it attach to the circle you drew for the body?

3 Start with the basic shapes of the head and tail. Then draw the shapes in the legs. Mink's whole body is on an angle, so her legs sit much higher on the page than her arms. Finish up with the left wing. It's tucked behind her neck.

4 Freeze frame! Add details to the face, talons to the wings, spikes to the spine, and bones to the wings. Draw a talon at the end of each wing bone. Then draw a curved guideline on the neck and erase any extra lines.

5 More details! Draw teeth in Mink's mouth and sharp spikes on her tail and head. Connect each wing talon with a scalloped line. Then take your time and draw the details in the feet. Are you ready to tackle the bones in the second wing? Go for it!

6 Clean up your lines and add scales. When you're ready, color Mink's scales in shades of light blue and white. Does her entire body shimmer like a snowstorm? Great!

WINTER

As an IceWing prince, Winter often feels pressure to rise in the rankings. But dragons, and drawings, don't have to be perfect to have heart. If fear of making a mistake is causing you to freeze, try drawing the messiest version of Winter you can on scrap paper first. And only give yourself two minutes to do it! You might be surprised by what you come up with.

1 Start by drawing a lima bean shape for the body. Then attach the basic shapes of the head, neck, and tail. Remember that IceWing tails narrow into a whip-thin tip.

2 Add the basic shapes of the wings. The right wing can be a quick "V" at this stage. Notice the way the tip of the left wing falls behind the head.

3 Build on the basics you sketched in the previous steps. Finish the wing bones and long, pointed elbows, as well as the starter shapes for the right wing. It's similar to the shape of the left wing. Then work on the face, horns, and ear.

4 Spot check! Are the proportions good? Erase any lines from the starter shapes you don't need and clean up the outlines. Then add long, sweeping lines to the wings to show where they bend.

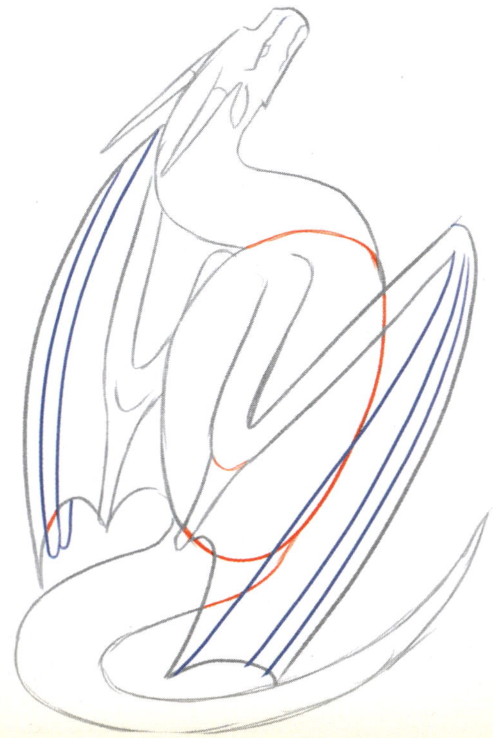

5 IceWings have lots of sharp edges and spikes. Draw them at the back of Winter's head and along his spine and tail. Then use curved lines to show off Winter's chest muscles and to make the tail look three-dimensional.

6 Refine the details in the face and body and use short, curved lines for Prince Winter's silvery and pale blue scales. Now that you can draw Winter, try drawing him using frostbreath to put out a fire at the Jade Mountain Academy!

UMBER

Clay's middle brother is loyal and kind to both his siblings and his winglet at the Jade Academy — just like a true MudWing! He often feels grateful that the War of SandWing Succession ended and the fighting between dragons stopped. What new drawing skills are you grateful for?

1 Umber's chest is proud, and his back is arched in this pose. Start by drawing a bean shape that is a little smaller on the bottom than the top.

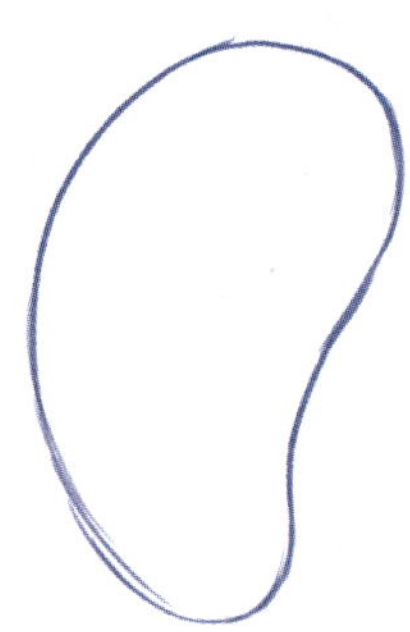

2 Attach the basic shapes of the head, neck, and tail. Remember that MudWings have blocky, rectangular heads.

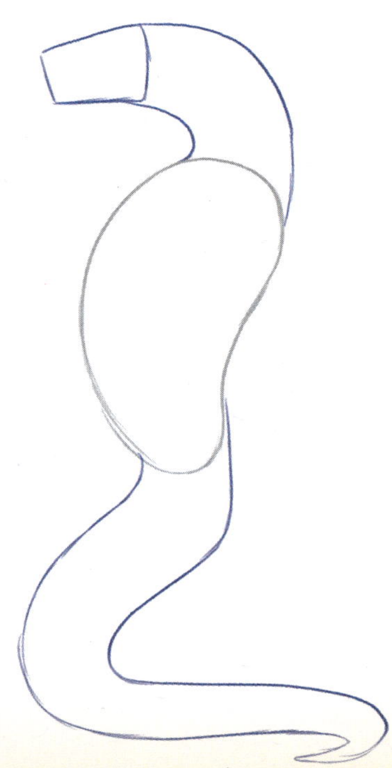

3 Draw Umber's wings, starting with the bones. Notice the "V" shape of the elbow. Umber's legs are hidden, but you can see the curve of the right leg peeking out where his tail meets the bean shape. One toe talon also sticks out from under the wing.

4 Clean up your lines and erase any you don't need. Then draw the facial features, horn, and ear. Do you see the curved line that runs from behind Umber's horn, across his neck, and down in front of the bean shape you drew for the body? Draw it now!

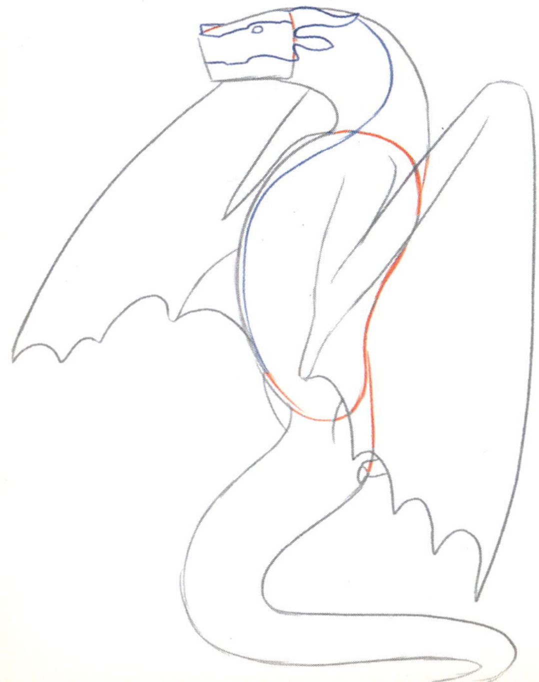

5 Draw feather-shaped spikes along the curved line you drew in step 4. Then finish the facial features and draw segment lines in the wings and a talon on the wingtip. Next, draw four curved lines — three in the tail and one on the chest.

6 Finish any details and start drawing Umber's thick, brown, armored scales. How many different shapes do you see in the scales? When you're done, try drawing Umber blending into a muddle puddle or breathing fire!

WILLOW

Willow may be a gentle LeafWing, but she can also act quickly when her friends are in danger. She stays calm and grounded even when new situations feel frustrating or scary. What are some strategies you can use to stay calm and keep moving when a drawing or part of a drawing feels frustrating?

1 Draw an egg shape for the body. It should sit at an angle with the smaller end pointing up and to the left.

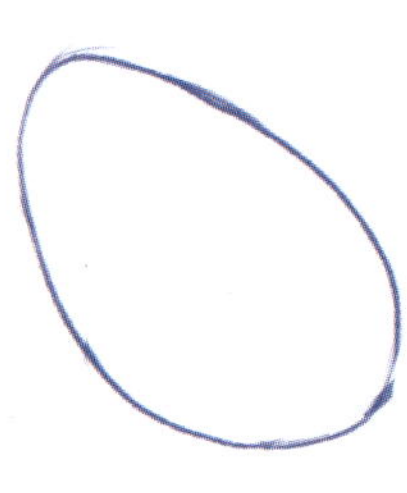

2 Draw a small circle above the oval, close to the right edge of the paper. Then connect the circle to the body with two curved lines for the neck.

3

Draw an oval for the arm inside the egg-shaped body. Then draw a line for the tail coming out of the underside of the body. Finish up by drawing the basic shape of Willow's snout.

4

Finish the arm with a circle for the shoulder and an oval for the forearm.

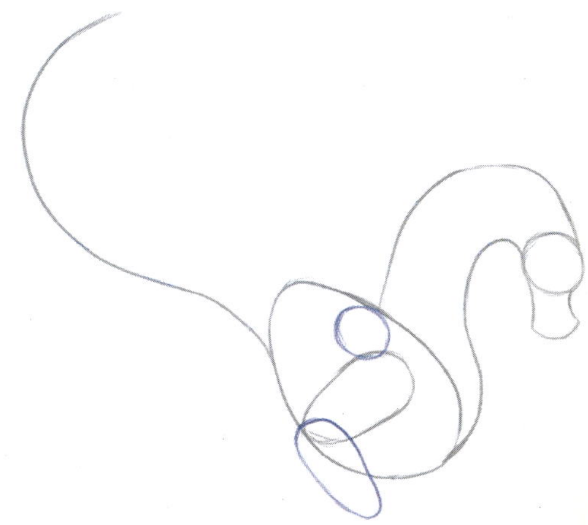

5

Keep building up the forms. Draw a simple hand. Then draw an upside-down egg behind the body on the tail. This will be the leg. Draw a bent line coming out of the shoulder circle for the wing bone. Then reshape the front of the chest.

6

Sketch in the basic shape of the left arm. Then continue building the right leg with an oval and a curved line.

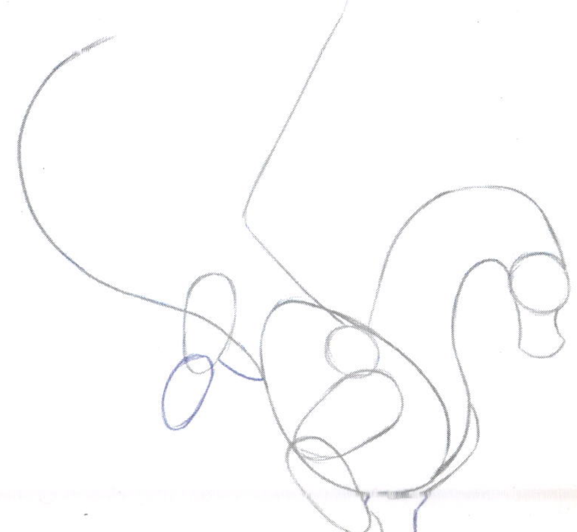

7 Add two wavy horns and an ear. Then it's wing time! Draw a gentle curve in front of the bent line you drew in step 5. Then draw a flowing curve like a butterfly wing that starts at the top of the bent line and ends at the bottom of the shoulder circle.

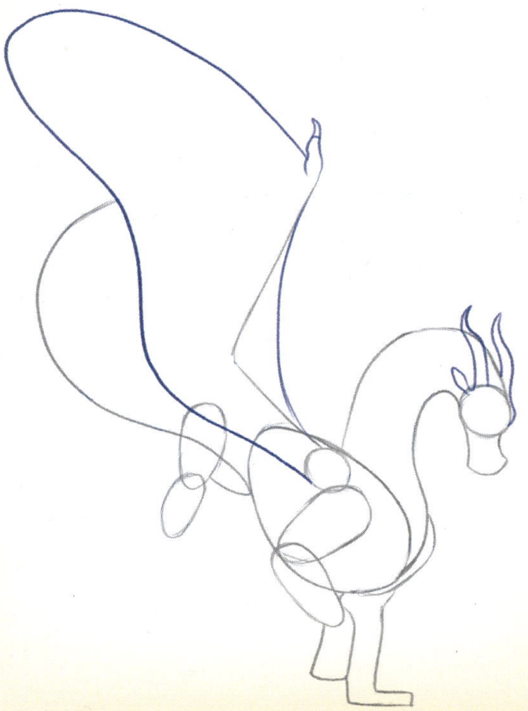

8 Use a curved line to finish the tail and another to draw the left wing. Add the basic shapes of the feet and draw the talons on the tips of the wings.

9 Need a breath of fresh air? Erase the guidelines you no longer need so you can see your drawing clearly. Are the wings similar in shape and scale? Does the right arm sit in front of the body?

10 Draw the right wing bone. Add a long, skinny talon at the elbow. Refine the shape of the shoulder. Then start adding facial features. The lines in Willow's face are long and elegant — just like she is!

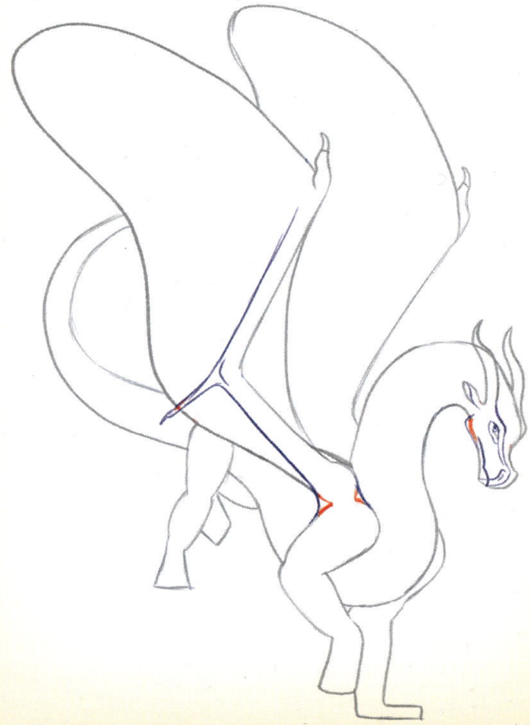

11 Draw a curved line on the neck that runs from the back of the ear to the top of the shoulder. Draw another small curve on the body from the armpit to the base of the wing.

12 Draw a "Y"-shaped wing bone inside the left wing. Work on the talons and refine the edges of the legs. Then draw two curves on the tail. A short line sits inside the spot where the tail curves.

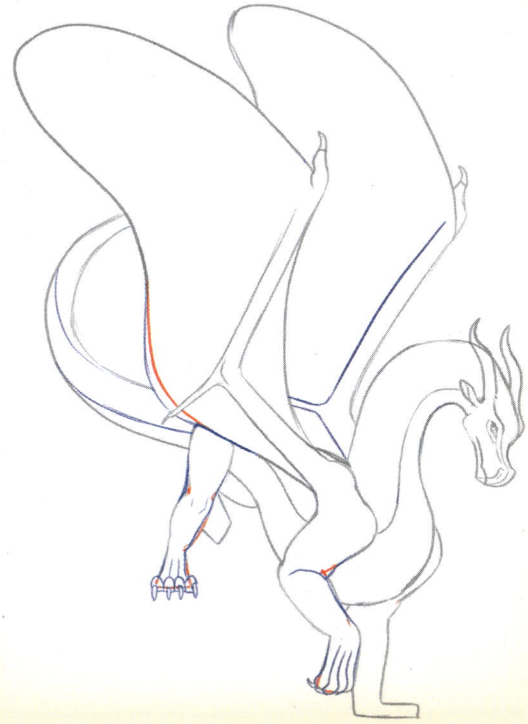

13 Ready to make your drawing look more like a LeafWing? Add a curve and fins to the back of her neck. Then finish drawing the rest of the talons and clean up the outlines.

14 Add horizontal lines to Willow's forehead, neck, and underbelly. Draw the decorative veins on Willow's wings. Sketch in some rounded scales. Then color her in soothing shades of pale green.

CRICKET

This HiveWing dragonet wants to understand the world around her. Cricket is obsessed with books, full of questions, and super curious about how things work and why they are the way they are. Need this drawing to make sense? Break each step down into smaller steps and take it line by line.

1 Draw a circle for the body and a rectangular shape for the head. The head should float at an angle above and to the left of the circle.

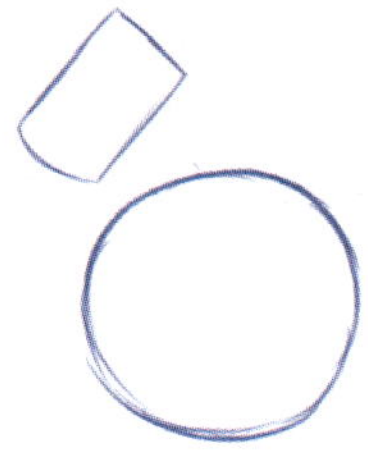

2 Draw the neck curving toward the left.

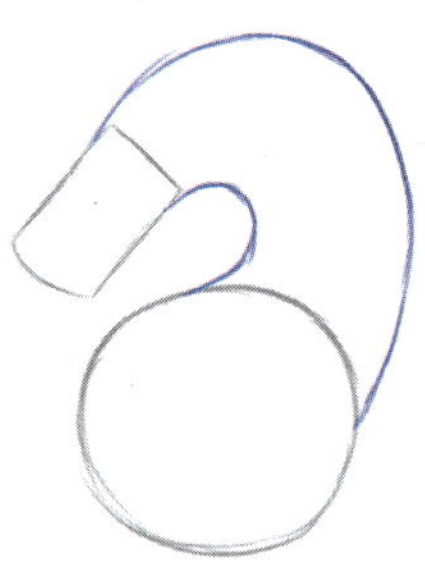

3 Sketch an oval on either side of the body for the upper arms. Then draw a curved line coming out of the bottom of each oval.

4 Finish the basic shapes of the left arm. Then draw two curved lines coming out the back of the shoulder circle. This is where you'll attach the left wing.

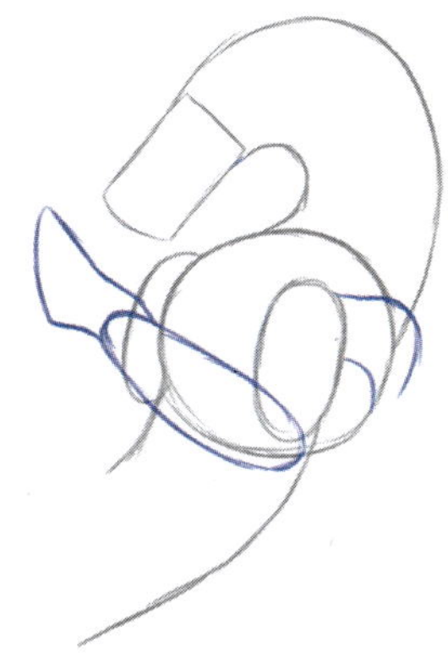

5 Draw an oval at the end of the two lines you drew in step 3. Then draw a bulblike shape for Cricket's right arm.

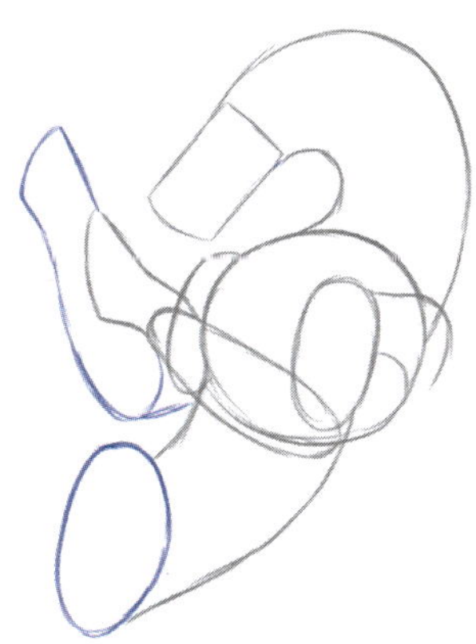

6 Draw a diamond shape on the left side of the oval you drew in step 5. Then draw an "S"-shaped line at the bottom of that oval for the tail. Jump up to the head and add horns, a squiggly mouth, and a short brow line that attaches to the ear.

7 Cricket is holding a book. For now, it looks like two triangles stuck together. Draw a tiny horn on the snout, and a curve like a lowercase "n" next to the diamond-shaped left foot. This will be the right knee. Then close off the right side of her tail.

8 Draw the outline of an eye and two ovals for glasses. Then work on the left leg. Start at the base of the diamond-shaped foot and draw a line that shoots up and curves in. Sketch in a similar curve on the right leg. Then draw the starter shapes for the right shin and foot.

9 Draw the outlines of all four wings. Notice where they connect to the body. Which wing do you think you should draw first? Why? Which wing comes next?

10 Take a break from the busy buzzing of lines and shapes. Erase any lines you no longer need. Adjust any lines that need to be fixed.

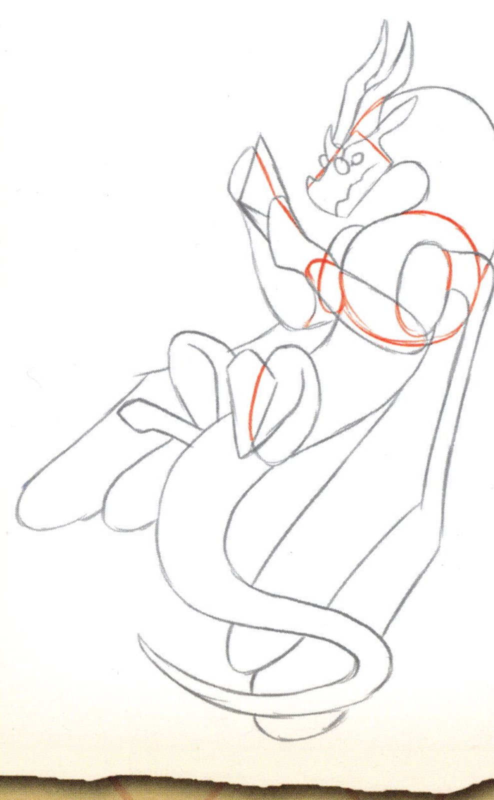

11 Draw the "T"-shape in the left wing and curved lines in the ear, the snout, and the end of the right arm. Then form the talons. Notice the way they curl around Cricket's book. How can you use the starter shapes to help you place each talon and claw?

12 We see the bottom of Cricket's foot in this pose. The perspective may be different, but the segments and lines are similar to the ones you've drawn before. When you're ready, draw lines that add dimension to the wings, snout, and belly.

13 Almost done! Draw the spikes on Cricket's spine and scales beside her eyes. Then use a combination of curved and straight lines to draw the detail in the wings.

14 What final moves do you need to make before your drawing feels done? Make them now! Then brighten up this drawing with color! Cricket's scales are orangey yellow and golden like the sun, with black specks like sunspots.

LUNA

This flamesilk dragonet is an artist at heart, but she's also an activist, determined to change the world for the better. And with her ability to spin fiery silk, she's uniquely suited to do it! What are your unique skills? What parts of the drawing process do you feel best at? What have you been surprised to learn about yourself as you draw the dragons in this book?

1 Draw an oval on an angle toward the left half of your paper. Then draw the basic shape of the head. It should float above the right side of the oval and face to the left.

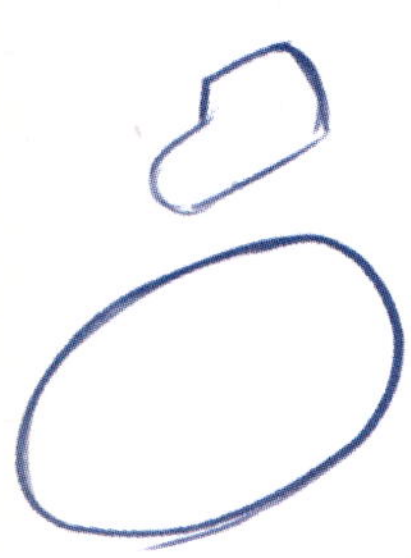

2 Connect the head and body with a short, curved neck. Then draw a quick line jutting out from the base of the neck. This will be the top of the wing.

3 Add two "V" shapes for the wing bones. Draw a slightly wavy line for the mouth.

4 Starting at the top of the oval, draw a long, sinewy line for the tail. Then sketch the back edge of the tail, making sure it runs parallel to the first line.

5 Starting at the underarm, draw a big "U" shape for the bottom of the wing. Allow the line to run right off the page. Draw a curve for the right leg at the front of the body. Then add a wavy horn and connect the brow line to it.

6 Draw two wavy antennae above Luna's horn. Then draw a curved line in front of her body that starts at the oval and runs up above her head. Finish up with a circular shape that touches both the wing and the tail.

7

Use curved lines to close off the top and bottom of the right wing. Draw another curve for the foot and one to show the bend of her left wing bone. Finish by drawing a curved line in the neck and the outline of her eye.

8

Pause. Are all the parts the right size and shape? Erase extra lines and tackle the facial features, horn, ear, and jawline. Draw a talon at the top of the wing bone and a long, narrow "V" shape at the elbow. Add curves and claws to the right foot.

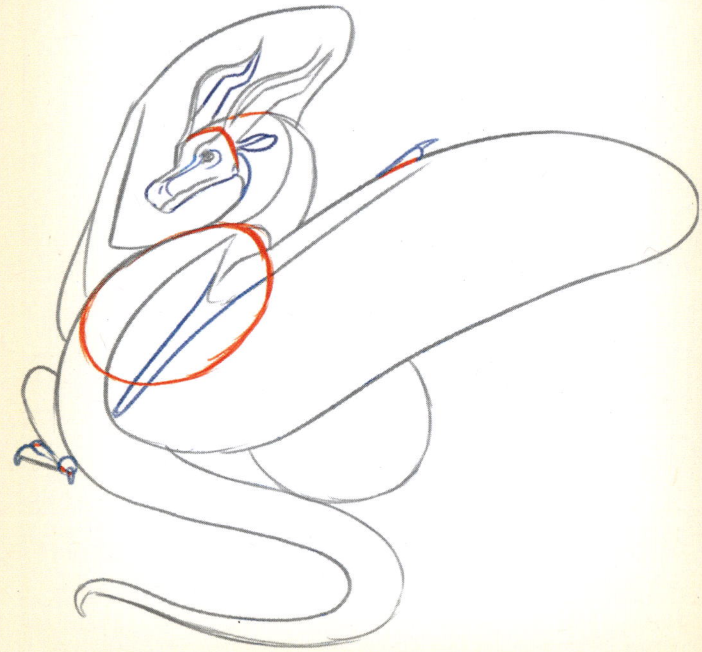

9

Add decorative elements like the paisley spots on Luna's wings and spikes along her spine. Add two curves to the wing and one to the tail.

10

Let this drawing take flight! Add the scales and the curved lines that add depth to the wings. Try using watercolors to give her pale green wings a sheer, glowing quality. Don't forget the gold flecks along her back and tail!

BLUE

Blue is not as bubbly or fierce as his sister, Luna, but he is just as determined to follow the rules in his heart — the ones that tell him to help other dragons and stand up for anyone who is being treated badly. Blue was born a SilkWing dragonet, so he hatched without wings — but don't worry, he'll grow them later during Metamorphosis!

1 Draw a large circle for the body. Then form a smaller circle for the backside. Connect them with a line that looks like half the letter "S."

2 Draw the outline of the head. Then draw a curved line for the bottom of the neck. Create a cluster of three small circles on the left side of the body circle. This will help you place the right arm and leg.

3 Attach two balloon-like shapes to the cluster of circles you drew in step 2. Then draw an oval above the spot where the neck meets the body. Attach the oval to the body with two curved lines. This will be the tail and left leg.

4 Finish the basic shapes of the left leg. Do you see how the curved line separates the leg into thigh, calf, and shin? Draw Blue's right knee with a curve like the lowercase letter "n." Don't forget the end of his tail. Do you see how it gets smaller as it moves into the distance? That's perspective!

5 Now sketch in the arms. Do you remember how you broke down the shapes when you drew Starflight's arms? Here's a tip: If you squint, you can see how the shapes crisscross like the letter "X."

6 Tackle this face head-on! Start with a squiggly line for the mouth and a teardrop for the eye. Then draw the two wiggly horns on top of Blue's head. See that line above the eye? It positions both the brow and the nostril — *and* sets the side of the face apart from the forehead and snout.

7 Pause to check your progress. Are you happy with the way all the shapes fit together? The front of Blue's body should look bigger than the back of his body because it is closer to you in space. Start erasing the red lines.

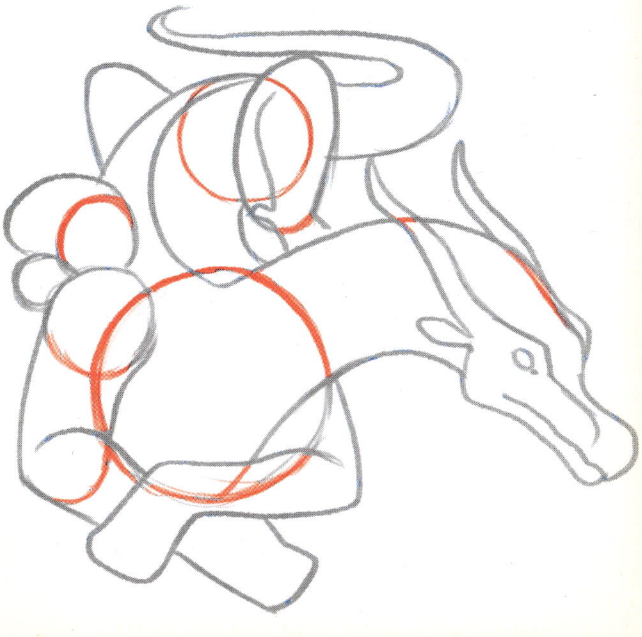

8 Draw the talons, antennae, and the curve inside the ear. The rest of the curved lines will help you draw spikes and scales in steps 9 and 10. Notice where each one starts and ends. Observe that they all follow the curves of the body.

9 Almost done! Add claws to Blue's talons and spikes to his spine. Start adding the decorative details on the side of his face. Draw two curves on each leg to define the knees.

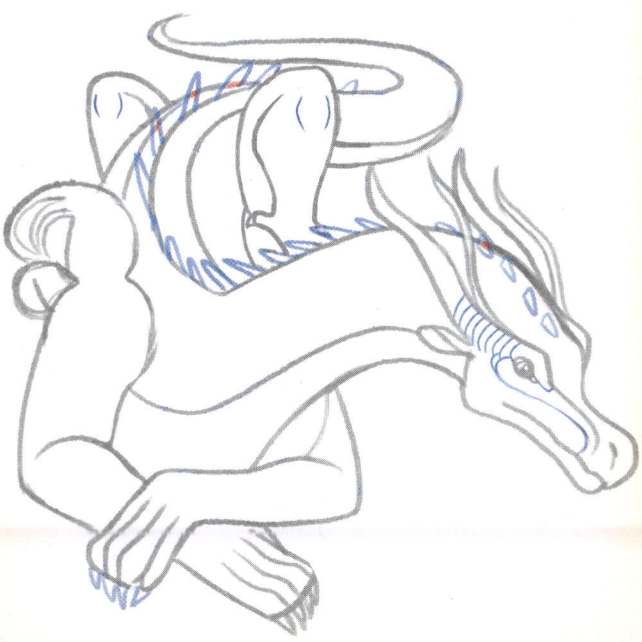

10 Get out your colors! Blue has gemlike scales in shades of blue, lavender, and purple. Color him with watercolors or markers for the most jewel-like tones. Then try using a thin black marker to get all the details in his scales.

SUNDEW

Sundew is a natural leader who acts like she's got everything figured out. She's brave, hot-tempered, *and* stubborn. Her lifelong mission has been to get revenge on the HiveWings for trying to wipe out the LeafWings. What's your mission with this drawing? Sundew is doing a nosedive in this picture. Sound like a fun pose to draw? Dive right in!

1 At the top of your page, draw the outline of a leaf. This is the tip of Sundew's tail. Then draw a jelly bean for the body. Because she's diving, you'll need to draw her head at the bottom of the paper.

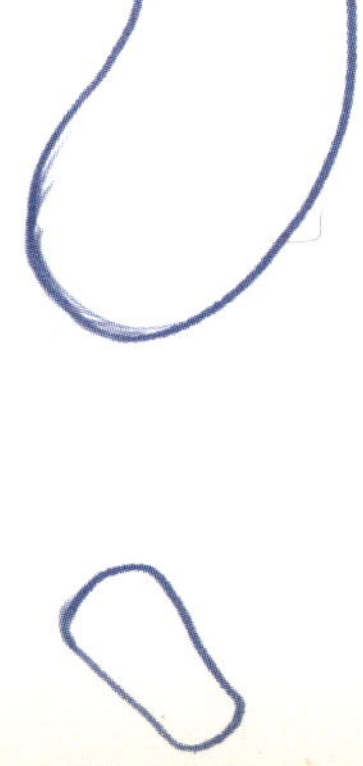

2 Draw Sundew's long, curved neck. Then draw an oval for her arm and two long starter shapes for the wings.

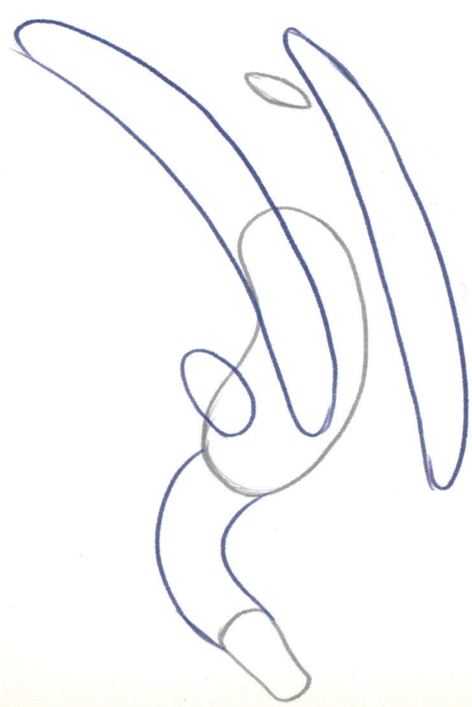

3 Break this step down into smaller steps. Start by drawing the swirling lines near the tail. Where do they overlap with the wings? When you're ready, draw the basic shapes of the arms, horns, eye, and ear. Don't forget the line between her back and her left wing.

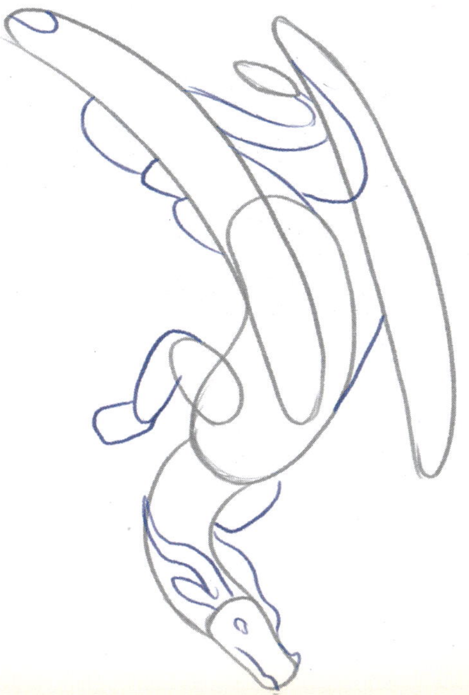

4 You're making so much progress! How does it feel? Erase the red lines. Are you starting to see which shapes sit in front of other shapes? Have the outlines of the tail become clearer?

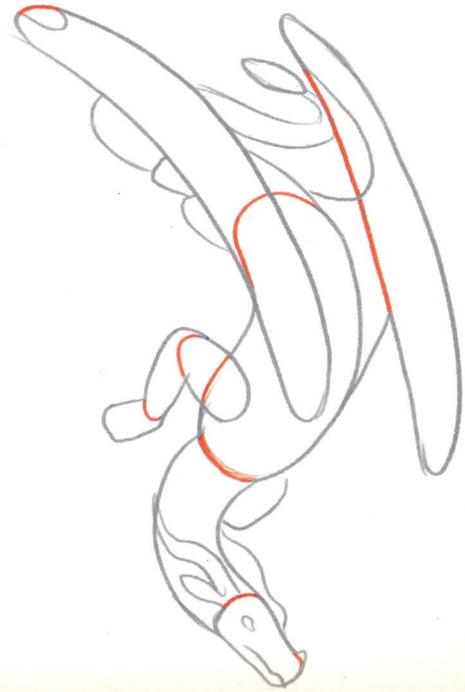

5 Draw the fins on Sundew's back, the talons on her hands and wings, and the details in her face. Reshape her arms and legs. Then take a closer look at the curves and lines in the wings. Some are scalloped edges. Others will become wing bones.

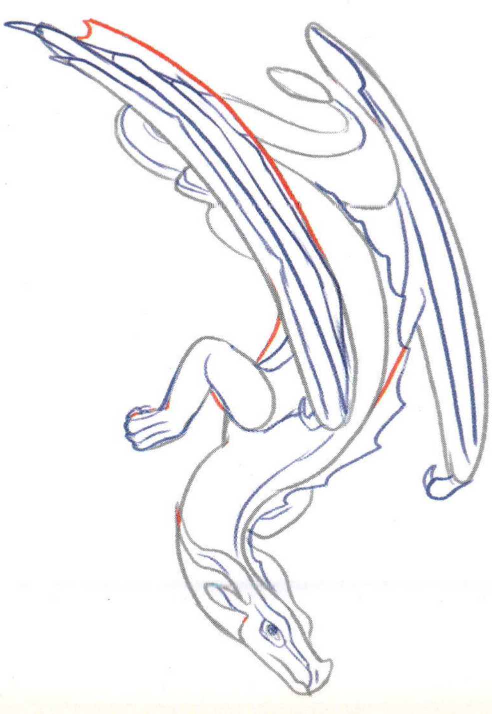

6 Tighten up the outlines of Sundew's body and add the final details to her fins, wings, and scales. Sundew wears many small pouches woven from long grass to hold her insects and plants. Draw them now!

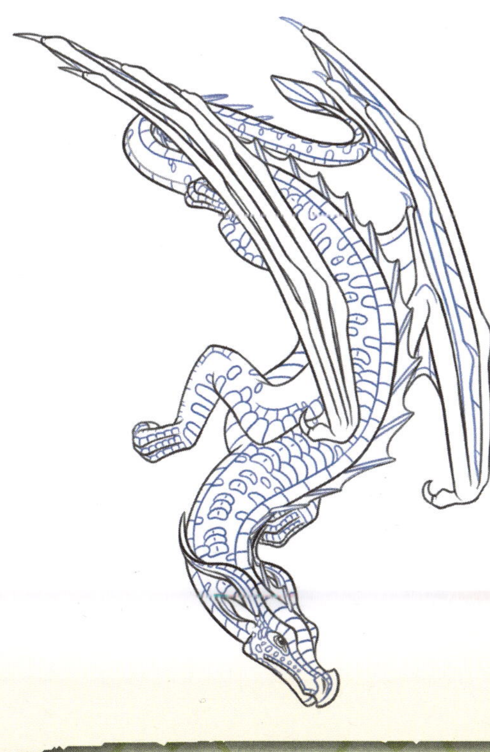

WASP

This queen has quite a sting! She used mind control to get the HiveWings to do her bidding — and plans to control the SilkWings, too! Want to take the sting out of this drawing? Set a timer for three minutes and draw Queen Wasp three times fast on scrap paper before you begin. You might be surprised to discover how much you've learned!

1 Start with a big circle for the body and a head that faces left. Then draw the neck and tail.

2 Wasp is formidable, so let's get her fierce face drawn first. Make sure you don't miss any of the spikes or horns on her head. Then draw two ovals for her legs.

3 Draw all four wasp wings. Notice where they connect to or overlap with the shapes and lines of the body. Then draw the basic shapes of the legs, the tip of the tail, and a circle for the shoulder.

4 You know the drill! Check your angles and proportions. Then erase the lines you no longer need.

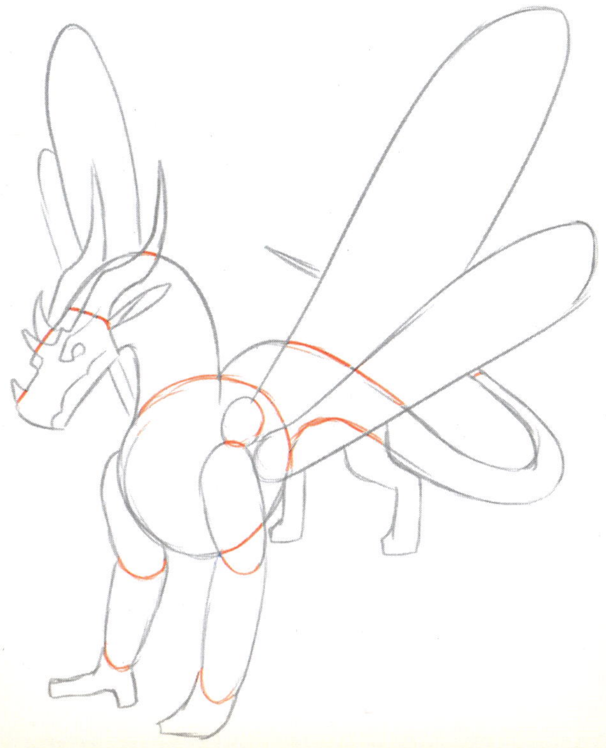

5 Deadly details! Add details to the face and talons, and draw the spikes that run along Wasp's spine. Then draw a few lines in the wings to give them structure.

6 Add the final details to Wasp's snarling mouth and yellow-and-black-striped body. Want to show the stingers extending from her claws? Draw them now!

SILVER

RainWings like Glory know life is better with friends, and many have a pet sloth to share their days — and lots of hugs! Warm up your drawing arm — and your heart — by sketching Glory's companion sloth, Silver.

1 Draw a basic tree trunk. Add an oval next to it. Then attach rounded arms and legs to the oval. Use a curved line for the head.

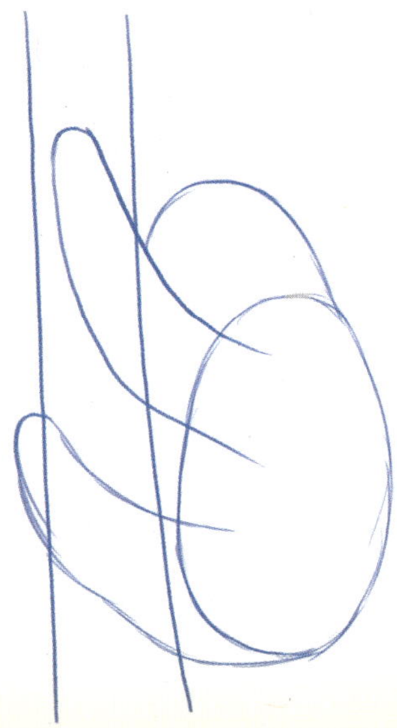

2 Draw two circles and two short lines for the right arm and leg. Add an oval for the snout and use it to place the facial features. Then erase the red guidelines.

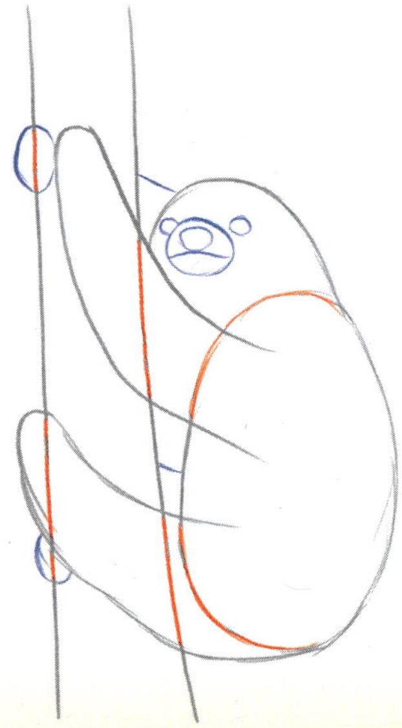

3 Ready to add details? Sloths have long nails like talons to grip trees and a mask like a raccoon.

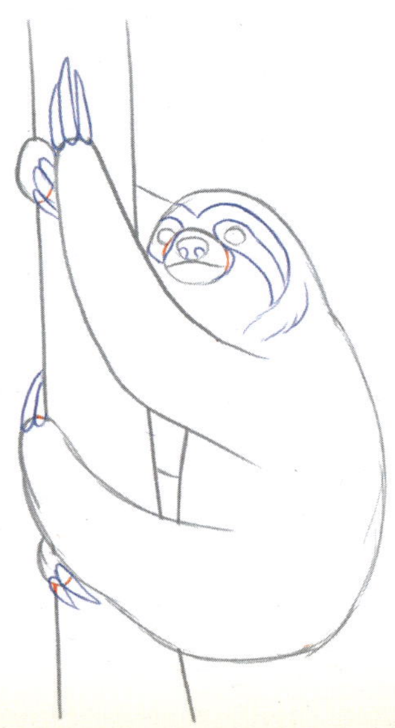

4 Use short hash marks for Silver's long, furry hair. Then get ready to color Silver in shades of Silver!